I0448272

MARCH 2013

Test Results for Digital Data Acquisition Tool:
X-Ways Forensics 14.8

NCJ 236224

Greg Ridgeway
Acting Director, National Institute of Justice

This report was prepared for the National Institute of Justice, U.S. Department of Justice, by the Office of Law Enforcement Standards of the National Institute of Standards and Technology under Interagency Agreement 2003–IJ–R–029.

The National Institute of Justice is a component of the Office of Justice Programs, which also includes the Bureau of Justice Assistance, the Bureau of Justice Statistics, the Office of Juvenile Justice and Delinquency Prevention, the Office for Victims of Crime, and the Office of Sex Offender Sentencing, Monitoring, Apprehending, Registering, and Tracking.

March 2013

Test Results for Digital Data Acquisition Tool:
X-Ways Forensics 14.8

**National Institute of
Standards and Technology**
U.S. Department of Commerce

Contents

Introduction

The Computer Forensics Tool Testing (CFTT) program is a joint project of the National Institute of Justice (NIJ), the research and development organization of the U.S. Department of Justice, and the National Institute of Standards and Technology's Law Enforcement Standards Office and Information Technology Laboratory. CFTT is supported by other organizations, including the Federal Bureau of Investigation, the U.S. Department of Defense Cyber Crime Center, the U.S. Internal Revenue Service Criminal Investigation Division Electronic Crimes Program, and the U.S. Department of Homeland Security's Bureau of Immigration and Customs Enforcement, U.S. Customs and Border Protection and U.S. Secret Service (USSS). The objective of the CFTT program is to provide measurable assurance to practitioners, researchers and other applicable users that the tools used in computer forensics investigations provide accurate results. Accomplishing this requires the development of specifications and test methods for computer forensics tools and subsequent testing of specific tools against those specifications.

Test results provide the information necessary for developers to improve tools, users to make informed choices, and the legal community and others to understand the tools' capabilities. The CFTT approach to testing computer forensic tools is based on well-recognized methodologies for conformance and quality testing. The specifications and test methods are posted on the CFTT Web site (http://www.cftt.nist.gov/) for review and comment by the computer forensics community.

This document reports the results from testing X-Ways Forensics, Version 14.8, against the *Digital Data Acquisition Tool Assertions and Test Plan Version 1.0*, available at the CFTT Web site (http://www.cftt.nist.gov/DA-ATP-pc-01.pdf).

Test results from other tools and the CFTT tool methodology can be found on NIJ's CFTT Web page, http://www.nij.gov/nij/topics/forensics/evidence/digital/standards/cftt.htm.

How to Read This Report

This report is divided into five sections. The first section is a summary of the results from the test runs and is sufficient for most readers to assess the suitability of the tool for the intended use. The remaining sections of the report describe how the tests were conducted, discuss any anomalies that were encountered and provide documentation of test case run details that support the report summary. Section 2 gives justification for the selection of test cases from the set of possible cases defined in the test plan for Digital Data Acquisition tools. The test cases are selected, in general, based on features offered by the tool. Section 3 describes in more depth any anomalies summarized in the first section. Section 4 lists hardware and software used to run the test cases, with links to additional information about the items used. Section 5 contains a description of each test case run. The description of each test run lists all test assertions used in the test case, the expected result and the actual result. For more information pertaining to the features and usage of X-Ways Forensics, see the vendor Web site (http://www.x-ways.com).

Test Results for Digital Data Acquisition Tool

Tool Tested: X-Ways Forensics
Version: 14.8
Run Environments: Windows: 2000 & XP

Supplier: X-Ways Software Technology AG

Address: X-Ways AG
                   Agrippastr. 37-39
                   50676 Cologne
                   Germany

Tel: +49 221-420 486 5
Fax: +49 3212-123 2029
Email: mail@x-ways.com
WWW: http://www.x-ways.com

1 Results Summary

The tool acquired source drives completely and accurately except for the cases where source drives containing faulty sectors were imaged, a logical NTFS partition was imaged, or a source drive containing hidden sectors, a *Host Protected Area* (HPA) or *Device Configuration Overlay* (DCO), was imaged. The tool restored image files and created clones accurately except for clone or restore operations on certain partitions and removable media where small changes to file system metadata were observed. The following anomalies were observed:

- Some readable sectors may be intentionally skipped, controlled by a parameter setting, to improve performance during acquisition of a drive with faulty sectors (DA-09-FW, DA-09-FW-XP and DA-09-USB).
- Eight unused sectors at the end of a partition containing an NT file system are not acquired (DA-07-NTFS). This is because the tool user selected acquiring the logical drive rather than the physical drive. If the physical drive is selected, all sectors of the partition should be acquired. This is not an issue with the tool; this result is noted to make the reader aware of the differences between choosing a logical vs. a physical acquisition.
- The tool does not acquire any sectors hidden by an HPA or a DCO. However, a separate tool, X-Ways Replica, can be used to remove an HPA or a DCO to make hidden sectors visible and then acquire the formerly hidden sectors (DA-08-ATA28, DA-08-ATA48 and DA-08-DCO).
- Small changes may be made by the operating system to file system metadata when cloning or restoring the image of a FAT32 or NTFS logical drive (DA-02-CF, DA-02-F32, DA-02-F32X, DA-14-CF, DA-14-F32, DA-14-F32X and DA-14-NTFS). The tool has no control over these changes.

- Only the first 268,435,456 sectors (128GB) of a drive larger than 128GB are acquired if the tool is executed in the Windows 2000 environment (DA-08-DCO). This is because of the limitations of Windows 2000 to handle drives requiring 48bit addressing. This is not an issue with the tool; this result is noted to make the reader aware of the consequences of operating system selection.

2 Test Case Selection

Test cases used to test disk imaging tools are defined in *Digital Data Acquisition Tool Assertions and Test Plan Version 1.0*. To test a tool, test cases are selected from the *Test Plan* document based on the features offered by the tool. Not all test cases or test assertions are appropriate for all tools. There is a core set of base cases (DA-06, DA-07 and DA-08) that are executed for every tool tested. Tool features guide the selection of additional test cases. If a given tool implements a given feature, then the test cases linked to that feature are run. Table 1 lists the features selected for testing and the linked test cases selected for execution. Table 2 lists the features not selected for testing and the test cases not executed.

Table 1 Selected Test Cases

Supported Optional Feature	Cases Selected for Execution
Base Cases	06, 07 & 08
Read error during acquisition	09
Create a clone from an image file	14 & 17
Destination Device Switching	13
Create a clone during acquisition	01
Create an unaligned clone from a digital source	02
Create a truncated clone from a physical device	04

Table 2 Omitted Test Cases

Unsupported Optional Feature	Cases Omitted (Not Executed)
Create cylinder aligned clones	03, 15, 21 & 23
Convert an image file from one format to another	26
Insufficient space for image file	12
Alternate image formats	10
Device I/O error generator available	05, 11 & 18
Fill excess sectors on a clone device	20, 21, 22 & 23
Create a clone from a subset of an image file	16
Fill excess sectors on a clone acquisition	19
Detect a corrupted (or changed) image file	24 & 25

Some test cases have variant forms to accommodate parameters within test assertions. These variant forms are designed to cover parameters that can vary within the test assertions. These variations cover the acquisition interface to the source drive (SRC-AI), the type of digital source (DS) object acquired, the execution environment (XE) and the way that sectors are hidden on a drive. Additional parameters that were varied between test cases and test case variations were types of hash algorithm calculated, image file segment size, the use of a hardware write blocker and the type of hardware write blocker used.

The following source access interfaces were tested: ATA28, ATA48, SATA28, SATA48, SCSI, FW, and USB. These are noted as variations on test cases DA-01, DA-06, DA-08 and DA-14.

The following digital sources were tested: partitions (FAT12, FAT16, FAT32, FAT32X, NTFS), compact flash (CF) and thumb drive (Thumb). There are two FAT 32 variations testing acquisition of both FAT 32 partition codes 0x0B (FAT32) and 0x0C (FAT32X). These digital source types are noted as variations on test cases DA-02 and DA-07.

Hardware write blockers were used in certain variations of the DA-01, DA-02, DA-07, DA-08 and DA-09 test cases.

3 Results by Test Assertion

A test assertion is a verifiable statement about a single condition after an action is performed by the tool under test. A test case usually checks a group of assertions after the action of a single execution of the tool under test. Test assertions are defined and linked to test cases in *Digital Data Acquisition Tool Assertions and Test Plan Version 1.0*. Table 3 summarizes the test results for all the test cases by assertion. The column labeled **Assertions Tested** gives the text of each assertion. The column labeled **Tests** gives the number of test cases that use the given assertion. The column labeled **Anomaly** gives the section number in this report where any observed anomalies are discussed.

See Section 2 for a discussion of source access interface, execution environment and digital source.

Table 3 Assertions Tested

Assertions Tested	Tests	Anomaly
AM-01 The tool uses access interface SRC-AI to access the digital source.	38	
AM-02 The tool acquires digital source DS.	38	
AM-03 The tool executes in execution environment XE.	53	
AM-04 If clone creation is specified, the tool creates a clone of the digital source.	13	
AM-05 If image file creation is specified, the tool creates an image file on file system type FS.	25	
AM-06 All visible sectors are acquired from the digital source.	38	3.3, 3.4, 3.5
AM-07 All hidden sectors are acquired from the digital source.	3	3.2

Assertions Tested	Tests	Anomaly
AM-08 All sectors acquired from the digital source are acquired accurately.	38	3.1
AM-09 If unresolved errors occur while reading from the selected digital source, the tool notifies the user of the error type and location within the digital source.	5	
AM-10 If unresolved errors occur while reading from the selected digital source, the tool uses a benign fill in the destination object in place of the inaccessible data.	5	
AO-01 If the tool creates an image file, the data represented by the image file is the same as the data acquired by the tool.	25	
AO-04 If the tool is creating an image file and there is insufficient space on the image destination device to contain the image file, the tool shall notify the user.	1	
AO-05 If the tool creates a multi-file image of a requested size, then all the individual files shall be no larger than the requested size.	25	
AO-10 If there is insufficient space to contain all files of a multi-file image, and if destination device switching is supported, the image is continued on another device.	1	
AO-11 If requested, a clone is created during an acquisition of a digital source.	13	
AO-12 If requested, a clone is created from an image file.	15	
AO-13 A clone is created using access interface DST-AI to write to the clone device.	28	
AO-14 If an unaligned clone is created, each sector written to the clone is accurately written to the same disk address on the clone that the sector occupied on the digital source.	27	3.1
AO-17 If requested, any excess sectors on a clone destination device are not modified.	12	
AO-19 If there is insufficient space to create a complete clone, a truncated clone is created using all available sectors of the clone device.	2	
AO-20 If a truncated clone is created, the tool notifies the user.	2	
AO-23 If the tool logs any log significant information, the information is accurately recorded in the log file.	53	
AO-24 If the tool executes in a forensically safe execution environment, the digital source is unchanged by the acquisition process.	38	

Table 4 Assertions Not Tested

Assertions Not Tested
AO-02 If an image file format is specified, the tool creates an image file in the specified format.
AO-03 If there is an error while writing the image file, the tool notifies the user.

Assertions Not Tested
AO-06 If the tool performs an image file integrity check on an image file that has not been changed since the file was created, the tool shall notify the user that the image file has not been changed.
AO-07 If the tool performs an image file integrity check on an image file that has been changed since the file was created, the tool shall notify the user that the image file has been changed.
AO-08 If the tool performs an image file integrity check on an image file that has been changed since the file was created, the tool shall notify the user of the affected locations.
AO-09 If the tool converts a source image file from one format to a target image file in another format, the acquired data represented in the target image file is the same as the acquired data in the source image file.
AO-15 If an aligned clone is created, each sector within a contiguous span of sectors from the source is accurately written to the same disk address on the clone device relative to the start of the span as the sector occupied on the original digital source. A span of sectors is defined to be either a mountable partition or a contiguous sequence of sectors not part of a mountable partition. Extended partitions, which may contain both mountable partitions and unallocated sectors, are not mountable partitions.
AO-16 If a subset of an image or acquisition is specified, all the subset is cloned.
AO-18 If requested, a benign fill is written to excess sectors of a clone.
AO-21 If there is a write error during clone creation, the tool notifies the user.
AO-22 If requested, the tool calculates block hashes for a specified block size during an acquisition for each block acquired from the digital source.

3.1 Metadata Changes During Restore or Clone

Small changes to file system metadata may occur when creating a clone or restoring the image of a FAT32 or NTFS logical drive. For FAT32 file systems, there are usually no more than three sectors with changes. The more intricate NTFS may have more than 200 sectors of metadata with at least one byte changed (DA-02-CF, DA-02-F32, DA-02-F32X, DA-14-CF, DA-14-F32, DA-14-F32X and DA-14-NTFS). These changes are made by the operating system. Sometimes the changes can be prevented by removing the device without following the normal shutdown procedure.

3.2 Acquisition of HPA and DCO

The tool does not remove an HPA or a DCO. The tool did not acquire sectors hidden by an HPA, or a DCO in test case DA-08 variations DA-08-DCO, DA-08-ATA28 and DA-08-ATA48. A separate tool, X-ways Replica, can be used to remove an HPA. The tool displays the following pop-up window if an HPA or a DCO is detected:

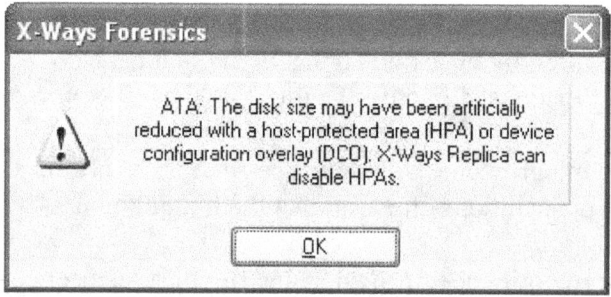

3.3 Logical Acquisition of NTFS Partition

Eight unused sectors at the end of a partition containing an NTFS file system are not acquired (DA-07-NTFS). The partition has 27,744,192 sectors but the tool acquires only 27,744,184 sectors, skipping the last eight sectors. However, the last eight sectors of an NT file system are not used to contain any user data. The eight sectors are omitted because the tool user selected acquiring the logical drive rather than the physical drive. If the physical drive is selected, all sectors of the partition should be acquired. This is not an issue with the tool; this result is noted to make the reader aware of the differences between choosing a logical vs. a physical acquisition.

3.4 Acquisition of 48bit Address Drive From Windows 2000

Only the first 268,435,456 sectors of a drive that requires 48bit addressing (i.e., larger than 128GB) are acquired if the tool is executed in the Windows 2000 environment (DA-08-DCO). Windows 2000 should not be used to acquire drives larger than 128GB.

3.5 Acquisition of Faulty Sectors

The tool allows the specification of a number of sectors to skip when a faulty sector is encountered. This feature improves tool performance, but some readable sectors are not acquired when the skip feature is used (DA-09-FW, DA-09-FW-XP and DA-09-USB).

4 Testing Environment

The tests were run in the NIST CFTT lab. This section describes the test computers available for testing, using the support software, and notes on other test hardware.

4.1 Test Computers

Three test computers were used.

Freddy, **Frank** and **Joe** have the following configuration:

Intel Desktop Motherboard D865GB/D865PERC (with ATA-6 IDE on board controller)
BIOS Version BF86510A.86A.0053.P13
Adaptec SCSI BIOS V3.10.0
Intel® Pentium™ 4 CPU 3.4Ghz
2577972KB RAM

SONY DVD RW DRU-530A, ATAPI CD/DVD-ROM drive
1.44 MB floppy drive
Two slots for removable IDE hard disk drives
Two slots for removable SATA hard disk drives
Two slots for removable SCSI hard disk drives

4.2 Support Software

A package of programs to support test analysis, FS-TST Release 2.0, was used. The software can be obtained from http://www.cftt.nist.gov/diskimaging/fs-tst20.zip.

4.3 Test Drive Creation

There are three ways that a hard drive may be used in a tool test case: as a source drive that is imaged by the tool, as a media drive that contains image files created by the tool under test, or as a destination drive on which the tool under test creates a clone of the source drive. In addition to the operating system drive formatting tools, some tools (**diskwipe** and **diskhash**) from the FS-TST package are used to set up test drives.

To set up a media drive, the drive is formatted with one of the supported file systems. A media drive may be used in several test cases.

The setup of most source drives follows the same general procedure, but there are several steps that may be varied depending on the needs of the test case.
1. The drive is filled with known data by the **diskwipe** program from FS-TST. The **diskwipe** program writes the sector address to each sector in both C/H/S and LBA format. The remainder of the sector bytes is set to a constant fill value unique for each drive. The fill value is noted in the **diskwipe** tool log file.
2. The drive may be formatted with partitions as required for the test case.
3. An operating system may optionally be installed.
4. A set of reference hashes is created by the FS-TST **diskhash** tool. These include both SHA1 and MD5 hashes. In addition to full drive hashes, hashes of each partition may also be computed.
5. If the drive is intended for hidden area tests (DA-08), an HPA, a DCO or both may be created. The **diskhash** tool is then used to calculate reference hashes of just the visible sectors of the drive.

The source drives for DA-09 are created such that there is a consistent set of faulty sectors on the drive. Each of these source drives is initialized with **diskwipe** and then their faulty sectors are activated. For each of these source drives, a second drive of the same size with the same content as the faulty sector drive but with no faulty sectors serves as a reference drive for images made from the faulty drive.

To set up a destination drive, the drive is filled with known data by the **diskwipe** program from FS-TST. Partitions may be created if the test case involves restoring from the image of a logical acquire.

4.4 Test Drive Analysis

For test cases that create a clone of a physical device (e.g., DA-01 and DA-04), the destination drive is compared to the source drive with the **diskcmp** program from the FS-TST package. For test cases that create a clone of a logical device (i.e., a partition, e.g., DA-02 and DA-20), the destination partition is compared to the source partition with the **partcmp** program. For a destination created from an image file (e.g., DA-14), the destination is compared, using either **diskcmp** (for physical device clones) or **partcmp** (for partition clones), to the source that was acquired to create the image file. Both **diskcmp** and **partcmp** note differences between the source and destination.

If the destination is larger than the source, then the excess destination sectors are categorized as either, undisturbed (still containing the fill pattern written by **diskwipe**), zero filled or changed to something else. A tool may provide a feature to wipe the excess sectors. For an FAT partition, the **diskcmp** and **partcmp** programs report the final state of the excess sectors. For an NTFS partition, metadata may be written to the excess sectors, overwriting the fill values placed by **diskwipe**. A special procedure is used to determine the state of excess sectors after restoring an NTFS partition, such as test case DA-14-NTFS. A destination drive is first pattern-filled with **diskwipe**, then, before restoring the partition, a hash is computed over the excess sectors on the destination. After the tool is used to restore the partition, another hash is computed over the excess sectors of the destination. If the two hashes match then none of the excess sectors have been changed by the tool.

For test case DA-09, imaging a drive with known faulty sectors, the program **anabad** is used to compare the faulty sector reference drive to a cloned version of the faulty sector drive.

For test cases such as DA-06 and DA-07, any acquisition hash computed by the tool under test is compared to the reference hash of the source to check that the source is completely and accurately acquired.

4.5 Comments on Test Drives

The testing uses several test drives from a variety of vendors. The drives are identified by an external label that consists of a 2-digit hexadecimal value and an optional tag (e.g., 25-SATA). The combination of hex value and tag serves as a unique identifier for each drive. The two digit hex value is used by the FS-TST **diskwipe** program as a sector fill value. The FS-TST compare tools, **diskcmp** and **partcmp**, count sectors that are filled with the source and destination fill values on a destination that is larger than the original source.

Table 5 lists the source test drives used. The models and serial numbers are listed as returned by the ATA IDENTIFY DEVICE command.

Table 5 Test Drives

Drive	Model	Serial #	Size (Sectors)
01-IDE	WDC WD400BB-00JHC0	WD-WMAMC7417100	78165360

Drive	Model	Serial #	Size (Sectors)
01-SATA	0JD-32HKA0	WD-WMAJ91448529	156301488
0B-SATA	00JD-22FYB0	WD-WMAEH2677545	488397168
43	0BB-75JHC0	WD-WMAMC46588	78125000
63-FU2	SP0612N	n/a	117304992
C1-CF	CF	n/a	503808
D5-THUMB	Usb2.0Flash Disk	n/a	505856
ED-BAD-CPR4	6Y060M0	Y23EGSJE	120103200
ED-BAD-CPR1	DiamondMax Plus 9	Y27KR6CE	120103200
24-FU2	ATCS04-0	CSH206D9DSEL	39070080
2D-IDE	WDC WD1600JB-00GVC0	WD-WMAL94887547	312581808
41	WDC WD400BB-75JHC0	WD-WMAMC4658355	78125000
4C	WDC WD2000JB-00KFA0	WD-WMAMR1031111	390721968
51-IDE	WDC WD1600JB-00GVC0	WD-WMAL94887547	312581808
7E	MAXTOR 6L040J2	662201136780	78177792
E0	ATLAS10K2-TY092J	169028142436	17938985

5 Test Results

The main item of interest for interpreting the test results is determining the conformance of the device with the test assertions. Conformance with each assertion tested by a given test case is evaluated by examining the **Log File Highlights** box of the test report summary.

5.1 Test Results Report Key

A summary of the actual test results is presented in this report. The following table presents a description of each section of the test report summary. The Tester Name, Test Host, Test Date, Drives, Source Setup and Log Highlights sections for each test case are populated by excerpts taken from the log files produced by the tool under test and the FS-TST tools that were executed in support of test case setup and analysis.

Heading	Description
First Line:	Test case ID, name and version of tool tested.
Case Summary:	Test case summary from *Digital Data Acquisition Tool Assertions and Test Plan Version 1.0*.
Assertions:	The test assertions applicable to the test case, selected from *Digital Data Acquisition Tool Assertions and Test Plan Version 1.0*.
Tester Name:	Name or initials of person executing test procedure.
Test Host:	Host computer executing the test.
Test Date:	Time and date that test was started.
Drives:	Source drive (the drive acquired), destination drive (if a clone is created) and media drive (to contain a created image).

Heading	Description
Source Setup:	Layout of partitions on the source drive and the expected hash of the drive.
Log Highlights:	Information extracted from various log files to illustrate conformance or non-conformance to the test assertions.
Results:	Expected and actual results for each assertion tested.
Analysis:	Whether or not the expected results were achieved.

5.2 Test Details

5.2.1 DA-01-ATA28

Test Case DA-01-ATA28 X-Ways 14.8	
Case Summary:	DA-01 Acquire a physical device using access interface AI to an unaligned clone.
Assertions:	AM-01 The tool uses access interface SRC-AI to access the digital source. AM-02 The tool acquires digital source DS. AM-03 The tool executes in execution environment XE. AM-04 If clone creation is specified, the tool creates a clone of the digital source. AM-06 All visible sectors are acquired from the digital source. AM-08 All sectors acquired from the digital source are acquired accurately. AO-11 If requested, a clone is created during an acquisition of a digital source. AO-13 A clone is created using access interface DST-AI to write to the clone device. AO-14 If an unaligned clone is created, each sector written to the clone is accurately written to the same disk address on the clone that the sector occupied on the digital source. AO-17 If requested, any excess sectors on a clone destination device are not modified. AO-22 If requested, the tool calculates block hashes for a specified block size during an acquisition for each block acquired from the digital source. AO-23 If the tool logs any log significant information, the information is accurately recorded in the log file. AO-24 If the tool executes in a forensically safe execution environment, the digital source is unchanged by the acquisition process.
Tester Name:	mrmw
Test Host:	Joe
Test Date:	Fri Jun 6 13:43:31 2008
Drives:	src(41) dst (F0) other (none)
Source Setup:	src hash (SHA256): < FBF3AA21489653D880FFAE71449A9F7E8EE4F56A6C3BF58A3A3FFB13203F1B1D > src hash (SHA1): < 15CAA1A307271160D8372668BF8A03FC45A51CC9 > src hash (MD5): < 0A6A8EF78BDC14E2026710D8CCB5607C > 78125000 total sectors (40000000000 bytes) 65534/015/63 (max cyl/hd values) 65535/016/63 (number of cyl/hd) IDE disk: Model (WDC WD400BB-75JHC0) serial # (WD-WMAMC4658355) N Start LBA Length Start C/H/S End C/H/S boot Partition type 1 P 000000063 078107967 0000/001/01 1023/254/63 Boot 07 NTFS 2 P 000000000 000000000 0000/000/00 0000/000/00 00 empty entry 3 P 000000000 000000000 0000/000/00 0000/000/00 00 empty entry 4 P 000000000 000000000 0000/000/00 0000/000/00 00 empty entry 1 078107967 sectors 39991279104 bytes
Log Highlights:	====== Destination drive setup ====== 156301488 sectors wiped with F0 ====== Comparison of original to clone drive ====== Sectors compared: 78125000 Sectors match: 78125000

```
                    Sectors differ:            0
                    Bytes differ:              0
                    Diffs range
                    Source (78125000) has 78176488 fewer sectors than destination (156301488)
                    Zero fill:                 0
                    Src Byte fill (41):        0
                    Dst Byte fill (F0): 78176488
                    Other fill:                0
                    Other no fill:             0
                    Zero fill range:
                    Src fill range:
                    Dst fill range:   78125000-156301487
                    Other fill range:
                    Other not filled range:
                    0 source read errors, 0 destination read errors


                    ====== Tool Settings: ======
                    simult yes
                    copy_entire yes
                    copy_portion NA
                    aviod_damage no
                    damage_skip_area NA
                    write_pattern_for_damage_area default
                    fill none

                    Write Block: 4 FastBloc IDE

                    ====== Extract from X-Ways log.txt file ======
                    Source device --> Destination device
                    WDC WD400BB-75JHC0 --> WDC WD800BB-00JHC0
                    78,125,000 sector(s) successfully copied.
```

	Assertion & Expected Result	Actual Result
Results:	AM-01 Source acquired using interface AI.	as expected
	AM-02 Source is type DS.	as expected
	AM-03 Execution environment is XE.	as expected
	AM-04 A clone is created.	as expected
	AM-06 All visible sectors acquired.	as expected
	AM-08 All sectors accurately acquired.	as expected
	AO-11 A clone is created during acquisition.	as expected
	AO-13 Clone created using interface AI.	as expected
	AO-14 An unaligned clone is created.	as expected
	AO-17 Excess sectors are unchanged.	as expected
	AO-22 Tool calculates hashes by block.	option not available
	AO-23 Logged information is correct.	as expected
	AO-24 Source is unchanged by acquisition.	not checked

Analysis:	Expected results achieved

5.2.2 DA-01-ATA48

Test Case DA-01-ATA48 X-Ways 14.8	
Case Summary:	DA-01 Acquire a physical device using access interface AI to an unaligned clone.
Assertions:	AM-01 The tool uses access interface SRC-AI to access the digital source. AM-02 The tool acquires digital source DS. AM-03 The tool executes in execution environment XE. AM-04 If clone creation is specified, the tool creates a clone of the digital source. AM-06 All visible sectors are acquired from the digital source. AM-08 All sectors acquired from the digital source are acquired accurately. AO-11 If requested, a clone is created during an acquisition of a digital source. AO-13 A clone is created using access interface DST-AI to write to the clone device. AO-14 If an unaligned clone is created, each sector written to the clone is accurately written to the same disk address on the clone that the sector occupied on the digital source. AO-17 If requested, any excess sectors on a clone destination device are not modified. AO-22 If requested, the tool calculates block hashes for a specified block size during an acquisition for each block acquired from the digital source. AO-23 If the tool logs any log significant information, the information is accurately recorded in the log file. AO-24 If the tool executes in a forensically safe execution environment, the digital source is unchanged by the acquisition process.
Tester Name:	mrmw
Test Host:	Frank
Test Date:	Fri Jun 20 16:06:27 2008
Drives:	src(4C) dst (29-IDE) other (none)
Source Setup:	src hash (SHA1): < 8FF620D2BEDCCAFE8412EDAAD56C8554F872EFBF > src hash (MD5): < D10F763B56D4CEBA2D1311C61F9FB382 > 390721968 total sectors (200049647616 bytes) 24320/254/63 (max cyl/hd values) 24321/255/63 (number of cyl/hd) IDE disk: Model (WDC WD2000JB-00KFA0) serial # (WD-WMAMR1031111) N Start LBA Length Start C/H/S End C/H/S boot Partition type 1 P 000000063 390700737 0000/001/01 1023/254/63 Boot 07 NTFS 2 P 000000000 000000000 0000/000/00 0000/000/00 00 empty entry 3 P 000000000 000000000 0000/000/00 0000/000/00 00 empty entry 4 P 000000000 000000000 0000/000/00 0000/000/00 00 empty entry 1 390700737 sectors 200038777344 bytes
Log Highlights:	====== Destination drive setup ====== 488397168 sectors wiped with 29 ====== Comparison of original to clone drive ====== Sectors compared: 390721968 Sectors match: 390721968 Sectors differ: 0 Bytes differ: 0 Diffs range Source (390721968) has 97675200 fewer sectors than destination (488397168) Zero fill: 0 Src Byte fill (4C): 0 Dst Byte fill (29): 97675200 Other fill: 0 Other no fill: 0 Zero fill range: Src fill range: Dst fill range: 390721968-488397167 Other fill range: Other not filled range: 0 source read errors, 0 destination read errors ====== Tool Settings: ======

```
                simult yes
                copy_entire yes
                copy_portion NA
                avoid_damage no
                damage_skip_area NA
                write_pattern_for_damage benign
                fill_pattern_for_damage NA
                fill none
                Write Block: 3 FastBloc IDE

                OS: Microsoft Windows XP [Version 5.1.2600]

                ====== Extract from X-Ways log.txt file ======
                Source device --> Destination device
                WDC WD2000JB-00KFA0 --> WDC WD2500JB-00GVC0
                390,721,968 sector(s) successfully copied.
```

Results:

Assertion & Expected Result	Actual Result
AM-01 Source acquired using interface AI.	as expected
AM-02 Source is type DS.	as expected
AM-03 Execution environment is XE.	as expected
AM-04 A clone is created.	as expected
AM-06 All visible sectors acquired.	as expected
AM-08 All sectors accurately acquired.	as expected
AO-11 A clone is created during acquisition.	as expected
AO-13 Clone created using interface AI.	as expected
AO-14 An unaligned clone is created.	as expected
AO-17 Excess sectors are unchanged.	as expected
AO-22 Tool calculates hashes by block.	option not available
AO-23 Logged information is correct.	as expected
AO-24 Source is unchanged by acquisition.	not checked

Analysis: Expected results achieved

5.2.3 DA-01-SATA28

Test Case DA-01-SATA28 X-Ways 14.8	
Case Summary:	DA-01 Acquire a physical device using access interface AI to an unaligned clone.
Assertions:	AM-01 The tool uses access interface SRC-AI to access the digital source. AM-02 The tool acquires digital source DS. AM-03 The tool executes in execution environment XE. AM-04 If clone creation is specified, the tool creates a clone of the digital source. AM-06 All visible sectors are acquired from the digital source. AM-08 All sectors acquired from the digital source are acquired accurately. AO-11 If requested, a clone is created during an acquisition of a digital source. AO-13 A clone is created using access interface DST-AI to write to the clone device. AO-14 If an unaligned clone is created, each sector written to the clone is accurately written to the same disk address on the clone that the sector occupied on the digital source. AO-17 If requested, any excess sectors on a clone destination device are not modified. AO-22 If requested, the tool calculates block hashes for a specified block size during an acquisition for each block acquired from the digital source. AO-23 If the tool logs any log significant information, the information is accurately recorded in the log file. AO-24 If the tool executes in a forensically safe execution environment, the digital source is unchanged by the acquisition process.
Tester Name:	mrmw
Test Host:	Frank
Test Date:	Wed Jun 25 12:06:34 2008
Drives:	src(01-sata) dst (32-sata) other (none)
Source Setup:	src hash (MD5): < 0A49B13D91FA9DA87CEEE9D006CB6FD6 > 156301488 total sectors (80026361856 bytes) Model (0JD-32HKA0) serial # (WD-WMAJ91448529)
Log Highlights:	====== Destination drive setup ====== 156301488 sectors wiped with 32 ====== Comparison of original to clone drive ====== Sectors compared: 156301488 Sectors match: 156301488 Sectors differ: 0 Bytes differ: 0 Diffs range 0 source read errors, 0 destination read errors ====== Tool Settings: ====== simult no copy_entire yes copy_portion NA avoid_damage no damage_skip_area NA write_pattern_for_damge default fill_pattern_for_damage NA fill none Write Block: none OS: Microsoft Windows XP [Version 5.1.2600] ====== Extract from X-Ways log.txt file ====== Source device --> Destination device WDC WD800JD-32HKA0 --> Hitachi HDS721680PLA380 156,301,488 sector(s) successfully copied.
Results:	

Assertion & Expected Result	Actual Result

Test Case DA-01-SATA28 X-Ways 14.8		
	AM-01 Source acquired using interface AI.	as expected
	AM-02 Source is type DS.	as expected
	AM-03 Execution environment is XE.	as expected
	AM-04 A clone is created.	as expected
	AM-06 All visible sectors acquired.	as expected
	AM-08 All sectors accurately acquired.	as expected
	AO-11 A clone is created during acquisition.	as expected
	AO-13 Clone created using interface AI.	as expected
	AO-14 An unaligned clone is created.	as expected
	AO-17 Excess sectors are unchanged.	as expected
	AO-22 Tool calculates hashes by block.	option not available
	AO-23 Logged information is correct.	as expected
	AO-24 Source is unchanged by acquisition.	as expected
Analysis:	Expected results achieved	

5.2.4 DA-01-SATA48

Test Case DA-01-SATA48 X-Ways 14.8	
Case Summary:	DA-01 Acquire a physical device using access interface AI to an unaligned clone.
Assertions:	AM-01 The tool uses access interface SRC-AI to access the digital source.
	AM-02 The tool acquires digital source DS.
	AM-03 The tool executes in execution environment XE.
	AM-04 If clone creation is specified, the tool creates a clone of the digital source.
	AM-06 All visible sectors are acquired from the digital source.
	AM-08 All sectors acquired from the digital source are acquired accurately.
	AO-11 If requested, a clone is created during an acquisition of a digital source.
	AO-13 A clone is created using access interface DST-AI to write to the clone device.
	AO-14 If an unaligned clone is created, each sector written to the clone is accurately written to the same disk address on the clone that the sector occupied on the digital source.
	AO-17 If requested, any excess sectors on a clone destination device are not modified.
	AO-22 If requested, the tool calculates block hashes for a specified block size during an acquisition for each block acquired from the digital source.
	AO-23 If the tool logs any log significant information, the informatin is accurately recorded in the log file.
	AO-24 If the tool executes in a forensically safe execution environment, the digital source is unchanged by the acquisition process.
Tester Name:	mrmw
Test Host:	Frank
Test Date:	Fri Jun 20 15:36:29 2008
Drives:	src(0B-SATA) dst (2C-SATA) other (none)
Source Setup:	src hash (SHA1): < >
	src hash (MD5): < 1873847F597A69D0F5DB991B67E84F92 >
	488397168 total sectors (250059350016 bytes)
	30400/254/63 (max cyl/hd values)
	30401/255/63 (number of cyl/hd)
	Model (00JD-22FYB0) serial # (WD-WMAEH2677545)
Log Highlights:	====== Destination drive setup ======
	488397168 sectors wiped with 1
	====== Comparison of original to clone drive ======
	Sectors compared: 488397168
	Sectors match: 488397168
	Sectors differ: 0
	Bytes differ: 0
	Diffs range
	0 source read errors, 0 destination read errors
	====== Tool Settings: ======
	simult no
	copy_entire yes
	copy_portion NA
	aviod_damage no
	damage_skip_area NA
	write_pattern_for_damage default
	fill_pattern_for_damage NA
	fill none
	Write Block: none
	OS: Microsoft Windows XP [Version 5.1.2600]
	====== Extract from X-Ways log.txt file ======
	Source device --> Destination device
	WDC WD2500JD-22FYB0 --> WDC WD2500AAKS-00VSA0
	488,397,168 sector(s) successfully copied.

Test Case DA-01-SATA48 X-Ways 14.8

Results:	

Assertion & Expected Result	Actual Result
AM-01 Source acquired using interface AI.	as expected
AM-02 Source is type DS.	as expected
AM-03 Execution environment is XE.	as expected
AM-04 A clone is created.	as expected
AM-06 All visible sectors acquired.	as expected
AM-08 All sectors accurately acquired.	as expected
AO-11 A clone is created during acquisition.	as expected
AO-13 Clone created using interface AI.	as expected
AO-14 An unaligned clone is created.	as expected
AO-17 Excess sectors are unchanged.	as expected
AO-22 Tool calculates hashes by block.	option not available
AO-23 Logged information is correct.	as expected
AO-24 Source is unchanged by acquisition.	as expected

Analysis:	Expected results achieved

5.2.5 DA-01-SCSI

Test Case DA-01-SCSI X-Ways 14.8	
Case Summary:	DA-01 Acquire a physical device using access interface AI to an unaligned clone.
Assertions:	AM-01 The tool uses access interface SRC-AI to access the digital source. AM-02 The tool acquires digital source DS. AM-03 The tool executes in execution environment XE. AM-04 If clone creation is specified, the tool creates a clone of the digital source. AM-06 All visible sectors are acquired from the digital source. AM-08 All sectors acquired from the digital source are acquired accurately. AO-11 If requested, a clone is created during an acquisition of a digital source. AO-13 A clone is created using access interface DST-AI to write to the clone device. AO-14 If an unaligned clone is created, each sector written to the clone is accurately written to the same disk address on the clone that the sector occupied on the digital source. AO-17 If requested, any excess sectors on a clone destination device are not modified. AO-22 If requested, the tool calculates block hashes for a specified block size during an acquisition for each block acquired from the digital source. AO-23 If the tool logs any log significant information, the information is accurately recorded in the log file. AO-24 If the tool executes in a forensically safe execution environment, the digital source is unchanged by the acquisition process.
Tester Name:	mrmw
Test Host:	Joe
Test Date:	Fri Jun 20 14:27:15 2008
Drives:	src(E0) dst (E3) other (none)
Source Setup:	src hash (SHA1): < 4A6941F1337A8A22B10FC844B4D7FA6158BECB82 > src hash (MD5): < A97C8F36B7AC9D5233B90AC09284F938 > 17938985 total sectors (9184760320 bytes) Model (ATLAS10K2-TY092J) serial # (169028142436)
Log Highlights:	====== Destination drive setup ====== 17938985 sectors wiped with E3 ====== Comparison of original to clone drive ====== Sectors compared: 17938985 Sectors match: 17938985 Sectors differ: 0 Bytes differ: 0 Diffs range 0 source read errors, 0 destination read errors ====== Tool Settings: ====== simult yes copy_entire yes copy_portion NA avoid_damage no damage_skip_area NA write_pattern_for_damage benign fill_pattern_for_damage NA fill none Write Block: none OS: Microsoft Windows [Version 5.2.3790] ====== Extract from X-Ways log.txt file ====== Source device --> Destination device QUANTUM ATLAS10K2-TY092J --> QUANTUM ATLAS10K2-TY092J 17,938,985 sector(s) successfully copied.
Results:	
	Assertion & Expected Result **Actual Result**

Test Case DA-01-SCSI X-Ways 14.8		
	AM-01 Source acquired using interface AI.	as expected
	AM-02 Source is type DS.	as expected
	AM-03 Execution environment is XE.	as expected
	AM-04 A clone is created.	as expected
	AM-06 All visible sectors acquired.	as expected
	AM-08 All sectors accurately acquired.	as expected
	AO-11 A clone is created during acquisition.	as expected
	AO-13 Clone created using interface AI.	as expected
	AO-14 An unaligned clone is created.	as expected
	AO-17 Excess sectors are unchanged.	as expected
	AO-22 Tool calculates hashes by block.	option not available
	AO-23 Logged information is correct.	as expected
	AO-24 Source is unchanged by acquisition.	as expected
Analysis:	Expected results achieved	

5.2.6 DA-01-USB

Test Case DA-01-USB X-Ways 14.8	
Case Summary:	DA-01 Acquire a physical device using access interface AI to an unaligned clone.
Assertions:	AM-01 The tool uses access interface SRC-AI to access the digital source. AM-02 The tool acquires digital source DS. AM-03 The tool executes in execution environment XE. AM-04 If clone creation is specified, the tool creates a clone of the digital source. AM-06 All visible sectors are acquired from the digital source. AM-08 All sectors acquired from the digital source are acquired accurately. AO-11 If requested, a clone is created during an acquisition of a digital source. AO-13 A clone is created using access interface DST-AI to write to the clone device. AO-14 If an unaligned clone is created, each sector written to the clone is accurately written to the same disk address on the clone that the sector occupied on the digital source. AO-17 If requested, any excess sectors on a clone destination device are not modified. AO-22 If requested, the tool calculates block hashes for a specified block size during an acquisition for each block acquired from the digital source. AO-23 If the tool logs any log significant information, the information is accurately recorded in the log file. AO-24 If the tool executes in a forensically safe execution environment, the digital source is unchanged by the acquisition process.
Tester Name:	mrmw
Test Host:	Frank
Test Date:	Mon Jun 30 07:08:19 2008
Drives:	src(63-FU2) dst (61-FU2) other (none)
Source Setup:	src hash (SHA256): < EC8EF011494BA6DA18F74C47547C3E74E7180585096A830F9247A98EF613BB1D > src hash (SHA1): < F7069EDCBEAC863C88DECED82159F22DA96BE99B > src hash (MD5): < EE217BC4FA4F3D1B4021D29B065AA9EC > 117304992 total sectors (60060155904 bytes) Model (SP0612N) serial # () N Start LBA Length Start C/H/S End C/H/S boot Partition type 1 P 000000063 004192902 0000/001/01 0260/254/63 Boot 06 Fat16 2 X 004192965 113097600 0261/000/01 1023/254/63 0F extended 3 S 000000063 113097537 0261/001/01 1023/254/63 0B Fat32 4 S 000000000 000000000 0000/000/00 0000/000/00 00 empty entry 5 P 000000000 000000000 0000/000/00 0000/000/00 00 empty entry 6 P 000000000 000000000 0000/000/00 0000/000/00 00 empty entry 1 004192902 sectors 2146765824 bytes 3 113097537 sectors 57905938944 bytes
Log Highlights:	====== Destination drive setup ====== 117304992 sectors wiped with 61 ====== Comparison of original to clone drive ====== Sectors compared: 117304992 Sectors match: 117304992 Sectors differ: 0 Bytes differ: 0 Diffs range 0 source read errors, 0 destination read errors ====== Tool Settings: ====== simult yes copy_entire yes copy_portion NA aviod_damage no damage_skip_area NA write_pattern_for_damage benign fill_pattern_for_damage NA

Test Case DA-01-USB X-Ways 14.8

```
fill none

Write Block: 18 UltraBlock-USB

OS: Microsoft Windows XP [Version 5.1.2600]

====== Extract from X-Ways log.txt file ======
Source device --> Destination device
SAMSUNG SP0612N --> SAMSUNG SP0612N
117,304,992 sector(s) successfully copied.
```

Results:

Assertion & Expected Result	Actual Result
AM-01 Source acquired using interface AI.	as expected
AM-02 Source is type DS.	as expected
AM-03 Execution environment is XE.	as expected
AM-04 A clone is created.	as expected
AM-06 All visible sectors acquired.	as expected
AM-08 All sectors accurately acquired.	as expected
AO-11 A clone is created during acquisition.	as expected
AO-13 Clone created using interface AI.	as expected
AO-14 An unaligned clone is created.	as expected
AO-17 Excess sectors are unchanged.	as expected
AO-22 Tool calculates hashes by block.	option not available
AO-23 Logged information is correct.	as expected
AO-24 Source is unchanged by acquisition.	not checked

Analysis: Expected results achieved

5.2.7 DA-02-CF

Test Case DA-02-CF X-Ways 14.8	
Case Summary:	DA-02 Acquire a digital source of type DS to an unaligned clone.
Assertions:	AM-01 The tool uses access interface SRC-AI to access the digital source. AM-02 The tool acquires digital source DS. AM-03 The tool executes in execution environment XE. AM-04 If clone creation is specified, the tool creates a clone of the digital source. AM-06 All visible sectors are acquired from the digital source. AM-08 All sectors acquired from the digital source are acquired accurately. AO-11 If requested, a clone is created during an acquisition of a digital source. AO-13 A clone is created using access interface DST-AI to write to the clone device. AO-14 If an unaligned clone is created, each sector written to the clone is accurately written to the same disk address on the clone that the sector occupied on the digital source. AO-17 If requested, any excess sectors on a clone destination device are not modified. AO-22 If requested, the tool calculates block hashes for a specified block size during an acquisition for each block acquired from the digital source. AO-23 If the tool logs any log significant information, the information is accurately recorded in the log file. AO-24 If the tool executes in a forensically safe execution environment, the digital source is unchanged by the acquisition process.
Tester Name:	mrmw
Test Host:	Frank
Test Date:	Tue Jul 1 08:04:41 2008
Drives:	src(C1-CF) dst (C2-CF) other (none)
Source Setup:	src hash (SHA256): < C7CF0218222DF80D5316511D6814266C7FA507C13F795AD3D323BB73C1590D80 > src hash (SHA1): < 5B8235178DF99FA307430C088F81746606638A0B > src hash (MD5): < 776DF8B4D2589E21DEBCF589EDC16D78 > 503808 total sectors (257949696 bytes) Model (CF) serial # () N Start LBA Length Start C/H/S End C/H/S boot Partition type 1 P 778135908 1141509631 0357/116/40 0357/032/45 Boot 72 other 2 P 168689522 1936028240 0288/115/43 0367/114/50 Boot 65 other 3 P 1869881465 1936028192 0366/032/33 0357/032/43 Boot 79 other 4 P 2885681152 000055499 0372/097/50 0000/010/00 Boot 0D other 1 1141509631 sectors 584452931072 bytes 2 1936028240 sectors 991246458880 bytes 3 1936028192 sectors 991246434304 bytes 4 000055499 sectors 28415488 bytes
Log Highlights:	====== Comparison of original to clone drive ====== Sectors compared: 503808 Sectors match: 503807 Sectors differ: 1 Bytes differ: 1 Diffs range 1 0 source read errors, 0 destination read errors Write Block: 7 Digital Intelligence UltraBlock Card Reader OS: Microsoft Windows 2000 [Version 5.00.2195] ====== Extract from X-Ways log.txt file ====== Source device --> Destination device ICSI CF Card CF --> USB2.0 HS-CF 503,808 sector(s) successfully copied.
Results:	
	Assertion & Expected Result **Actual Result**

Test Case DA-02-CF X-Ways 14.8		
	AM-01 Source acquired using interface AI.	as expected
	AM-02 Source is type DS.	as expected
	AM-03 Execution environment is XE.	as expected
	AM-04 A clone is created.	as expected
	AM-06 All visible sectors acquired.	as expected
	AM-08 All sectors accurately acquired.	one sector differs
	AO-11 A clone is created during acquisition.	as expected
	AO-13 Clone created using interface AI.	as expected
	AO-14 An unaligned clone is created.	as expected
	AO-17 Excess sectors are unchanged.	as expected
	AO-22 Tool calculates hashes by block.	option not available
	AO-23 Logged information is correct.	as expected
	AO-24 Source is unchanged by acquisition.	not checked
Analysis:	Expected results not achieved	

5.2.8 DA-02-F12

Test Case DA-02-F12 X-Ways 14.8	
Case Summary:	DA-02 Acquire a digital source of type DS to an unaligned clone.
Assertions:	AM-01 The tool uses access interface SRC-AI to access the digital source. AM-02 The tool acquires digital source DS. AM-03 The tool executes in execution environment XE. AM-04 If clone creation is specified, the tool creates a clone of the digital source. AM-06 All visible sectors are acquired from the digital source. AM-08 All sectors acquired from the digital source are acquired accurately. AO-11 If requested, a clone is created during an acquisition of a digital source. AO-13 A clone is created using access interface DST-AI to write to the clone device. AO-14 If an unaligned clone is created, each sector written to the clone is accurately written to the same disk address on the clone that the sector occupied on the digital source. AO-17 If requested, any excess sectors on a clone destination device are not modified. AO-22 If requested, the tool calculates block hashes for a specified block size during an acquisition for each block acquired from the digital source. AO-23 If the tool logs any log significant information, the informaion is accurately recorded in the log file. AO-24 If the tool executes in a forensically safe execution environment, the digital source is unchanged by the acquisition process.
Tester Name:	brl
Test Host:	Freddy
Test Date:	Thu Feb 24 10:23:51 2011
Drives:	src(01-IDE) dst (24-SATA) other (none)

Source Setup:	src hash (SHA1): < A48BB5665D6DC57C22DB68E2F723DA9AA8DF82B9 >
	src hash (MD5): < F458F673894753FA6A0EC8B8EC63848E >
	78165360 total sectors (40020664320 bytes)
	Model (0BB-00JHC0) serial # (WD-WMAMC74171)
	  N Start LBA Length Start C/H/S End C/H/S boot Partition type
	  1 P 000000063 020980827 0000/001/01 1023/254/63 0C Fat32X
	  2 X 020980890 057175335 1023/000/01 1023/254/63 0F extended
	  3 S 000000063 000032067 1023/001/01 1023/254/63 01 Fat12
	  4 x 000032130 002104515 1023/000/01 1023/254/63 05 extended
	  5 S 000000063 002104452 1023/001/01 1023/254/63 06 Fat16
	  6 x 002136645 004192965 1023/000/01 1023/254/63 05 extended
	  7 S 000000063 004192902 1023/001/01 1023/254/63 16 other
	  8 x 006329610 008401995 1023/000/01 1023/254/63 05 extended
	  9 S 000000063 008401932 1023/001/01 1023/254/63 0B Fat32
	 10 x 014731605 010490445 1023/000/01 1023/254/63 05 extended
	 11 S 000000063 010490382 1023/001/01 1023/254/63 83 Linux
	 12 x 025222050 004209030 1023/000/01 1023/254/63 05 extended
	 13 S 000000063 004208967 1023/001/01 1023/254/63 82 Linux swap
	 14 x 029431080 027744255 1023/000/01 1023/254/63 05 extended
	 15 S 000000063 027744192 1023/001/01 1023/254/63 07 NTFS
	 16 S 000000000 000000000 0000/000/00 0000/000/00 00 empty entry
	 17 P 000000000 000000000 0000/000/00 0000/000/00 00 empty entry
	 18 P 000000000 000000000 0000/000/00 0000/000/00 00 empty entry
	 1 020980827 sectors 10742183424 bytes
	 3 000032067 sectors 16418304 bytes
	 5 002104452 sectors 1077479424 bytes
	 7 004192902 sectors 2146765824 bytes
	 9 008401932 sectors 4301789184 bytes
	 11 010490382 sectors 5371075584 bytes
	 13 004208967 sectors 2154991104 bytes
	 15 027744192 sectors 14205026304 bytes
	 01F12-md5 16418303 E20E3CFEA80BF6F2D2AA75E829CC8CD9
	 01F12-sha1 16418303 F8B72B65436DE3BD394ACFF71D405D0389C0E9B7

Log Highlights:	====== Destination drive setup ====== 156301488 sectors wiped with 24

```
Test Case DA-02-F12 X-Ways 14.8
             ====== Comparison of original to clone drive ======
             Sectors compared:       32067
             Sectors match:          32067
             Sectors differ:             0
             Bytes differ:               0
             Diffs range:
             run start Thu Feb 24 11:37:06 2011
             run finish Thu Feb 24 11:37:08 2011
             elapsed time 0:0:2
             Normal exit

             Write Block: 57 Tableau T35e

             OS: Microsoft Windows XP [Version 5.1.2600]

             ====== Extract from X-Ways log.txt file ======
             Source device --> Destination device
             Drive N: --> Drive E:
             32,067 sector(s) successfully copied.
```

Assertion & Expected Result	Actual Result
AM-01 Source acquired using interface AI.	as expected
AM-02 Source is type DS.	as expected
AM-03 Execution environment is XE.	as expected
AM-04 A clone is created.	as expected
AM-06 All visible sectors acquired.	as expected
AM-08 All sectors accurately acquired.	as expected
AO-11 A clone is created during acquisition.	as expected
AO-13 Clone created using interface AI.	as expected
AO-14 An unaligned clone is created.	as expected
AO-17 Excess sectors are unchanged.	as expected
AO-22 Tool calculates hashes by block.	option not available
AO-23 Logged information is correct.	as expected
AO-24 Source is unchanged by acquisition.	not checked

Results: (left label)

Analysis: Expected results achieved

5.2.9 DA-02-F16

Test Case DA-02-F16 X-Ways 14.8	
Case Summary:	DA-02 Acquire a digital source of type DS to an unaligned clone.
Assertions:	AM-01 The tool uses access interface SRC-AI to access the digital source. AM-02 The tool acquires digital source DS. AM-03 The tool executes in execution environment XE. AM-04 If clone creation is specified, the tool creates a clone of the digital source. AM-06 All visible sectors are acquired from the digital source. AM-08 All sectors acquired from the digital source are acquired accurately. AO-11 If requested, a clone is created during an acquisition of a digital source. AO-13 A clone is created using access interface DST-AI to write to the clone device. AO-14 If an unaligned clone is created, each sector written to the clone is accurately written to the same disk address on the clone that the sector occupied on the digital source. AO-17 If requested, any excess sectors on a clone destination device are not modified. AO-22 If requested, the tool calculates block hashes for a specified block size during an acquisition for each block acquired from the digital source. AO-23 If the tool logs any log significant information, the information is accurately recorded in the log file. AO-24 If the tool executes in a forensically safe execution environment, the digital source is unchanged by the acquisition process.
Tester Name:	brl
Test Host:	Freddy
Test Date:	Wed Oct 20 11:33:30 2010
Drives:	src(43) dst (07-IDE) other (none)

Source Setup:	src hash (SHA256): <
	2658F47603DE6B1D883B64823E9733F578658D08D06A4BB8C053C4F57BDC615E >
	src hash (SHA1): < 888E2E7F7AD237DC7A732281DD93F325065E5871 >
	src hash (MD5): < BC39C3F7EE7A50E77B9BA1E65A5AEEF7 >
	78125000 total sectors (40000000000 bytes)
	Model (0BB-75JHC0) serial # (WD-WMAMC46588)
	<pre> N Start LBA Length Start C/H/S End C/H/S boot Partition type
	  1 P 000000063 020980827 0000/001/01 1023/254/63 0C Fat32X
	  2 X 020980890 057143205 1023/000/01 1023/254/63 0F extended
	  3 S 000000063 000032067 1023/001/01 1023/254/63 01 Fat12
	  4 x 000032130 002104515 1023/000/01 1023/254/63 05 extended
	  5 S 000000063 002104452 1023/001/01 1023/254/63 06 Fat16
	  6 x 002136645 004192965 1023/000/01 1023/254/63 05 extended
	  7 S 000000063 004192902 1023/001/01 1023/254/63 16 other
	  8 x 006329610 008401995 1023/000/01 1023/254/63 05 extended
	  9 S 000000063 008401932 1023/001/01 1023/254/63 0B Fat32
	 10 x 014731605 010490445 1023/000/01 1023/254/63 05 extended
	 11 S 000000063 010490382 1023/001/01 1023/254/63 83 Linux
	 12 x 025222050 004209030 1023/000/01 1023/254/63 05 extended
	 13 S 000000063 004208967 1023/001/01 1023/254/63 82 Linux swap
	 14 x 029431080 027712125 1023/000/01 1023/254/63 05 extended
	 15 S 000000063 027712062 1023/001/01 1023/254/63 07 NTFS
	 16 S 000000000 000000000 0000/000/00 0000/000/00 00 empty entry
	 17 P 000000000 000000000 0000/000/00 0000/000/00 00 empty entry
	 18 P 000000000 000000000 0000/000/00 0000/000/00 00 empty entry
	 1 020980827 sectors 10742183424 bytes
	 3 000032067 sectors 16418304 bytes
	 5 002104452 sectors 1077479424 bytes
	 7 004192902 sectors 2146765824 bytes
	 9 008401932 sectors 4301789184 bytes
	11 010490382 sectors 5371075584 bytes
	13 004208967 sectors 2154991104 bytes
	15 027712062 sectors 14188575744 bytes</pre>43F16-md5sum 1077479423 37E81FFB31C3CB38AA48B2237500908E
	43F16-sha1sum 1077479423 443CCEC9A22F726DAF6CE384817151C83B3EBC8B

Log Highlights:	====== Destination drive setup ====== 40000464 sectors wiped with 7 ====== Comparison of original to clone drive ====== Sectors compared: 2104452 Sectors match: 2104452 Sectors differ: 0 Bytes differ: 0 Diffs range: Source (2104452) has 96390 fewer sectors than destination (2200842) Zero fill: 0 Src Byte fill (43): 0 Dst Byte fill (07): 96390 Other fill: 0 Other no fill: 0 Zero fill range: Src fill range: Dst fill range: 2104452-2200841 Other fill range: Other not filled range: run start Thu Oct 21 15:09:35 2010 run finish Thu Oct 21 15:12:17 2010 elapsed time 0:2:42 Normal exit Write Block: 57 Tableau T35e OS: Microsoft Windows 2000 [Version 5.00.2195] ====== Extract from X-Ways log.txt file ====== Source device --> Destination device Drive K: --> Drive G: 2,104,452 sector(s) successfully copied.
Results:	

Assertion & Expected Result	Actual Result
AM-01 Source acquired using interface AI.	as expected
AM-02 Source is type DS.	as expected
AM-03 Execution environment is XE.	as expected
AM-04 A clone is created.	as expected
AM-06 All visible sectors acquired.	as expected
AM-08 All sectors accurately acquired.	as expected
AO-11 A clone is created during acquisition.	as expected
AO-13 Clone created using interface AI.	as expected
AO-14 An unaligned clone is created.	as expected
AO-17 Excess sectors are unchanged.	as expected
AO-22 Tool calculates hashes by block.	option not available
AO-23 Logged information is correct.	as expected
AO-24 Source is unchanged by acquisition.	not checked

Analysis:	Expected results achieved

5.2.10   DA-02-F32

Test Case DA-02-F32 X-Ways 14.8	
Case Summary:	DA-02 Acquire a digital source of type DS to an unaligned clone.
Assertions:	AM-01 The tool uses access interface SRC-AI to access the digital source. AM-02 The tool acquires digital source DS. AM-03 The tool executes in execution environment XE. AM-04 If clone creation is specified, the tool creates a clone of the digital source. AM-06 All visible sectors are acquired from the digital source. AM-08 All sectors acquired from the digital source are acquired accurately. AO-11 If requested, a clone is created during an acquisition of a digital source. AO-13 A clone is created using access interface DST-AI to write to the clone device. AO-14 If an unaligned clone is created, each sector written to the clone is accurately written to the same disk address on the clone that the sector occupied on the digital source. AO-17 If requested, any excess sectors on a clone destination device are not modified. AO-22 If requested, the tool calculates block hashes for a specified block size during an acquisition for each block acquired from the digital source. AO-23 If the tool logs any log significant information, the information is accurately recorded in the log file. AO-24 If the tool executes in a forensically safe execution environment, the digital source is unchanged by the acquisition process.
Tester Name:	brl
Test Host:	Freddy
Test Date:	Thu Feb 24 14:18:02 2011
Drives:	src(01-IDE) dst (24-SATA) other (none)

Source Setup:	src hash (SHA1): < A48BB5665D6DC57C22DB68E2F723DA9AA8DF82B9 >
	src hash (MD5): < F458F673894753FA6A0EC8B8EC63848E >
	78165360 total sectors (40020664320 bytes)
	Model (0BB-00JHC0) serial # (WD-WMAMC74171)
	<pre>N Start LBA Length Start C/H/S End C/H/S boot Partition type
	 1 P 000000063 020980827 0000/001/01 1023/254/63 0C Fat32X
	 2 X 020980890 057175335 1023/000/01 1023/254/63 0F extended
	 3 S 000000063 000032067 1023/001/01 1023/254/63 01 Fat12
	 4 x 000032130 002104515 1023/000/01 1023/254/63 05 extended
	 5 S 000000063 002104452 1023/001/01 1023/254/63 06 Fat16
	 6 x 002136645 004192965 1023/000/01 1023/254/63 05 extended
	 7 S 000000063 004192902 1023/001/01 1023/254/63 16 other
	 8 x 006329610 008401995 1023/000/01 1023/254/63 05 extended
	 9 S 000000063 008401932 1023/001/01 1023/254/63 0B Fat32
	10 x 014731605 010490445 1023/000/01 1023/254/63 05 extended
	11 S 000000063 010490382 1023/001/01 1023/254/63 83 Linux
	12 x 025222050 004209030 1023/000/01 1023/254/63 05 extended
	13 S 000000063 004208967 1023/001/01 1023/254/63 82 Linux swap
	14 x 029431080 027744255 1023/000/01 1023/254/63 05 extended
	15 S 000000063 027744192 1023/001/01 1023/254/63 07 NTFS
	16 S 000000000 000000000 0000/000/00 0000/000/00 00 empty entry
	17 P 000000000 000000000 0000/000/00 0000/000/00 00 empty entry
	18 P 000000000 000000000 0000/000/00 0000/000/00 00 empty entry
	 1 020980827 sectors 10742183424 bytes
	 3 000032067 sectors 16418304 bytes
	 5 002104452 sectors 1077479424 bytes
	 7 004192902 sectors 2146765824 bytes
	 9 008401932 sectors 4301789184 bytes
	11 010490382 sectors 5371075584 bytes
	13 004208967 sectors 2154991104 bytes
	15 027744192 sectors 14205026304 bytes
	01F32-md5 4301789183 BFF7DC64C54339DA2A9D7972C076B514
	01F32-sha1 4301789183 B861D9E999F39750B484FFB693FF69DEC090C6B8</pre>

Log Highlights:	====== Destination drive setup ====== 156301488 sectors wiped with 24

Test Case DA-02-F32 X-Ways 14.8	
	====== Comparison of original to clone drive ====== Sectors compared: 8401932 Sectors match: 8401929 Sectors differ: 3 Bytes differ: 3 Diffs range: 1, 36, 8226 run start Thu Feb 24 14:59:47 2011 run finish Thu Feb 24 15:03:10 2011 elapsed time 0:3:23 Normal exit Write Block: 61 WiebeTech Forensic Ultradock4 OS: Microsoft Windows XP [Version 5.1.2600] ====== Extract from X-Ways log.txt file ====== Source device --> Destination device Drive L: --> Drive G: 8,401,932 sector(s) successfully copied.
Results:	

Assertion & Expected Result	Actual Result
AM-01 Source acquired using interface AI.	as expected
AM-02 Source is type DS.	as expected
AM-03 Execution environment is XE.	as expected
AM-04 A clone is created.	as expected
AM-06 All visible sectors acquired.	as expected
AM-08 All sectors accurately acquired.	three sectors differ
AO-11 A clone is created during acquisition.	as expected
AO-13 Clone created using interface AI.	as expected
AO-14 An unaligned clone is created.	as expected
AO-17 Excess sectors are unchanged.	as expected
AO-22 Tool calculates hashes by block.	option not available
AO-23 Logged information is correct.	as expected
AO-24 Source is unchanged by acquisition.	not checked

Analysis:	Expected results not achieved

5.2.11 DA-02-F32X

Test Case DA-02-F32X X-Ways 14.8	
Case Summary:	DA-02 Acquire a digital source of type DS to an unaligned clone.
Assertions:	AM-01 The tool uses access interface SRC-AI to access the digital source. AM-02 The tool acquires digital source DS. AM-03 The tool executes in execution environment XE. AM-04 If clone creation is specified, the tool creates a clone of the digital source. AM-06 All visible sectors are acquired from the digital source. AM-08 All sectors acquired from the digital source are acquired accurately. AO-11 If requested, a clone is created during an acquisition of a digital source. AO-13 A clone is created using access interface DST-AI to write to the clone device. AO-14 If an unaligned clone is created, each sector written to the clone is accurately written to the same disk address on the clone that the sector occupied on the digital source. AO-17 If requested, any excess sectors on a clone destination device are not modified. AO-22 If requested, the tool calculates block hashes for a specified block size during an acquisition for each block acquired from the digital source. AO-23 If the tool logs any log significant information, the informsation is accurately recorded in the log file. AO-24 If the tool executes in a forensically safe execution environment, the digital source is unchanged by the acquisition process.
Tester Name:	brl
Test Host:	Freddy
Test Date:	Thu Feb 24 15:10:39 2011
Drives:	src(01-IDE) dst (24-SATA) other (none)
Source Setup:	src hash (SHA1): < A48BB5665D6DC57C22DB68E2F723DA9AA8DF82B9 > src hash (MD5): < F458F673894753FA6A0EC8B8EC63848E > 78165360 total sectors (40020664320 bytes) Model (0BB-00JHC0) serial # (WD-WMAMC74171) N Start LBA Length Start C/H/S End C/H/S boot Partition type 1 P 000000063 020980827 0000/001/01 1023/254/63 0C Fat32X 2 X 020980890 057175335 1023/000/01 1023/254/63 0F extended 3 S 000000063 000032067 1023/001/01 1023/254/63 01 Fat12 4 x 000032130 002104515 1023/000/01 1023/254/63 05 extended 5 S 000000063 002104452 1023/001/01 1023/254/63 06 Fat16 6 x 002136645 004192965 1023/000/01 1023/254/63 05 extended 7 S 000000063 004192902 1023/001/01 1023/254/63 16 other 8 x 006329610 008401995 1023/000/01 1023/254/63 05 extended 9 S 000000063 008401932 1023/001/01 1023/254/63 0B Fat32 10 x 014731605 010490445 1023/000/01 1023/254/63 05 extended 11 S 000000063 010490382 1023/001/01 1023/254/63 83 Linux 12 x 025222050 004209030 1023/000/01 1023/254/63 05 extended 13 S 000000063 004208967 1023/001/01 1023/254/63 82 Linux swap 14 x 029431080 027744255 1023/000/01 1023/254/63 05 extended 15 S 000000063 027744192 1023/001/01 1023/254/63 07 NTFS 16 S 000000000 000000000 0000/000/00 0000/000/00 00 empty entry 17 P 000000000 000000000 0000/000/00 0000/000/00 00 empty entry 18 P 000000000 000000000 0000/000/00 0000/000/00 00 empty entry 1 020980827 sectors 10742183424 bytes 3 000032067 sectors 16418304 bytes 5 002104452 sectors 1077479424 bytes 7 004192902 sectors 2146765824 bytes 9 008401932 sectors 4301789184 bytes 11 010490382 sectors 5371075584 bytes 13 004208967 sectors 2154991104 bytes 15 027744192 sectors 14205026304 bytes 01F32X-md5 10742183423 B5BFD9CE3990C577EF89C5AFB925F947 01F32X-sha1 10742183423 30BA6CF583A176C5DB533E3A2F57BFD5A4A870C1
Log Highlights:	====== Destination drive setup ====== 156301488 sectors wiped with 24

```
====== Comparison of original to clone drive ======
Sectors compared:     20980827
Sectors match:        20980824
Sectors differ:              3
Bytes differ:                3
Diffs range: 1, 32, 10268
Source (20980827) has 1558305 fewer sectors than destination (22539132)
Zero fill:      0
Src Byte fill (01): 0
Dst Byte fill (24): 1558305
Other fill:      0
Other no fill: 0
Zero fill range:
Src fill range:
Dst fill range:  20980827-22539131
Other fill range:
Other not filled range:
run start Thu Feb 24 15:38:29 2011
run finish Thu Feb 24 15:47:07 2011
elapsed time 0:8:38
Normal exit

Write Block: 61 WiebeTech Forensic Ultradock4

OS: Microsoft Windows XP [Version 5.1.2600]

====== Extract from X-Ways log.txt file ======
Source device --> Destination device
Drive O: --> Drive C:
20,980,827 sector(s) successfully copied.
```

Results:		
	Assertion & Expected Result	**Actual Result**
	AM-01 Source acquired using interface AI.	as expected
	AM-02 Source is type DS.	as expected
	AM-03 Execution environment is XE.	as expected
	AM-04 A clone is created.	as expected
	AM-06 All visible sectors acquired.	as expected
	AM-08 All sectors accurately acquired.	three sectors differ
	AO-11 A clone is created during acquisition.	as expected
	AO-13 Clone created using interface AI.	as expected
	AO-14 An unaligned clone is created.	as expected
	AO-17 Excess sectors are unchanged.	as expected
	AO-22 Tool calculates hashes by block.	option not available
	AO-23 Logged information is correct.	as expected
	AO-24 Source is unchanged by acquisition.	not checked

Analysis:	Expected results not achieved

5.2.12   DA-02-THUMB

Test Case DA-02-THUMB X-Ways 14.8	
Case Summary:	DA-02 Acquire a digital source of type DS to an unaligned clone.
Assertions:	AM-01 The tool uses access interface SRC-AI to access the digital source. AM-02 The tool acquires digital source DS. AM-03 The tool executes in execution environment XE. AM-04 If clone creation is specified, the tool creates a clone of the digital source. AM-06 All visible sectors are acquired from the digital source. AM-08 All sectors acquired from the digital source are acquired accurately. AO-11 If requested, a clone is created during an acquisition of a digital source. AO-13 A clone is created using access interface DST-AI to write to the clone device. AO-14 If an unaligned clone is created, each sector written to the clone is accurately written to the same disk address on the clone that the sector occupied on the digital source. AO-17 If requested, any excess sectors on a clone destination device are not modified. AO-22 If requested, the tool calculates block hashes for a specified block size during an acquisition for each block acquired from the digital source. AO-23 If the tool logs any log significant information, the information is accurately recorded in the log file. AO-24 If the tool executes in a forensically safe execution environment, the digital source is unchanged by the acquisition process.
Tester Name:	brl
Test Host:	Freddy
Test Date:	Thu Feb 10 14:49:23 2011
Drives:	src(D5-THUMB) dst (D6-THUMB) other (none)
Source Setup:	src hash (SHA1): < D68520EF74A336E49DCCF83815B7B08FDC53E38A > src hash (MD5): < C843593624B2B3B878596D8760B19954 > 505856 total sectors (258998272 bytes) Model (usb2.0Flash Disk) serial # ()
Log Highlights:	====== Destination drive setup ====== 4001760 sectors wiped with D6 ====== Comparison of original to clone drive ====== Sectors compared: 505856 Sectors match: 505856 Sectors differ: 0 Bytes differ: 0 Diffs range Source (505856) has 3495904 fewer sectors than destination (4001760) Zero fill: 0 Src Byte fill (D5): 0 Dst Byte fill (D6): 3495904 Other fill: 0 Other no fill: 0 Zero fill range: Src fill range: Dst fill range: 505856-4001759 Other fill range: Other not filled range: 0 source read errors, 0 destination read errors Write Block: 18 Tableau Forensic USB Bridge ====== Extract from X-Ways log.txt file ====== Source device --> Destination device CRUCIAL usb2.0Flash Disk --> SanDisk Cruzer Titanium 505,856 sector(s) successfully copied.
Results:	

Assertion & Expected Result	Actual Result
AM-01 Source acquired using interface AI.	as expected

Test Case DA-02-THUMB X-Ways 14.8		
	AM-02 Source is type DS.	as expected
	AM-03 Execution environment is XE.	as expected
	AM-04 A clone is created.	as expected
	AM-06 All visible sectors acquired.	as expected
	AM-08 All sectors accurately acquired.	as expected
	AO-11 A clone is created during acquisition.	as expected
	AO-13 Clone created using interface AI.	as expected
	AO-14 An unaligned clone is created.	as expected
	AO-17 Excess sectors are unchanged.	as expected
	AO-22 Tool calculates hashes by block.	option not available
	AO-23 Logged information is correct.	as expected
	AO-24 Source is unchanged by acquisition.	not checked
Analysis:	Expected results achieved	

5.2.13 DA-04

Test Case DA-04 X-Ways 14.8	
Case Summary:	DA-04 Acquire a physical device to a truncated clone.
Assertions:	AM-01 The tool uses access interface SRC-AI to access the digital source. AM-02 The tool acquires digital source DS. AM-03 The tool executes in execution environment XE. AM-04 If clone creation is specified, the tool creates a clone of the digital source. AM-06 All visible sectors are acquired from the digital source. AM-08 All sectors acquired from the digital source are acquired accurately. AO-11 If requested, a clone is created during an acquisition of a digital source. AO-13 A clone is created using access interface DST-AI to write to the clone device. AO-14 If an unaligned clone is created, each sector written to the clone is accurately written to the same disk address on the clone that the sector occupied on the digital source. AO-19 If there is insufficient space to create a complete clone, a truncated clone is created using all available sectors of the clone device. AO-20 If a truncated clone is created, the tool notifies the user. AO-22 If requested, the tool calculates block hashes for a specified block size during an acquisition for each block acquired from the digital source. AO-23 If the tool logs any log significant information, the information is accurately recorded in the log file. AO-24 If the tool executes in a forensically safe execution environment, the digital source is unchanged by the acquisition process.
Tester Name:	mrmw
Test Host:	Joe
Test Date:	Mon Jul 28 13:33:30 2008
Drives:	src(41) dst (69) other (none)
Source Setup:	src hash (SHA256): < FBF3AA21489653D880FFAE71449A9F7E8EE4F56A6C3BF58A3A3FFB13203F1B1D > src hash (SHA1): < 15CAA1A307271160D8372668BF8A03FC45A51CC9 > src hash (MD5): < 0A6A8EF78BDC14E2026710D8CCB5607C > 78125000 total sectors (40000000000 bytes) 65534/015/63 (max cyl/hd values) 65535/016/63 (number of cyl/hd) IDE disk: Model (WDC WD400BB-75JHC0) serial # (WD-WMAMC4658355) N Start LBA Length Start C/H/S End C/H/S boot Partition type 1 P 000000063 078107967 0000/001/01 1023/254/63 Boot 07 NTFS 2 P 000000000 000000000 0000/000/00 0000/000/00 00 empty entry 3 P 000000000 000000000 0000/000/00 0000/000/00 00 empty entry 4 P 000000000 000000000 0000/000/00 0000/000/00 00 empty entry 1 078107967 sectors 39991279104 bytes
Log Highlights:	====== Destination drive setup ====== 19925880 sectors wiped with 69 Write Block: 32 Tableau T5 ====== No X-Ways log.txt file created ======
Results:	Assertion & Expected Result	Actual Result

Test Case DA-04 X-Ways 14.8	
AM-01 Source acquired using interface AI.	as expected
AM-02 Source is type DS.	as expected
AM-03 Execution environment is XE.	as expected
AM-04 A clone is created.	as expected
AM-06 All visible sectors acquired.	as expected
AM-08 All sectors accurately acquired.	as expected
AO-11 A clone is created during acquisition.	as expected
AO-13 Clone created using interface AI.	as expected
AO-14 An unaligned clone is created.	as expected
AO-19 Truncated clone is created.	as expected
AO-20 User notified that clone is truncated.	as expected
AO-22 Tool calculates hashes by block.	option not available
AO-23 Logged information is correct.	as expected
AO-24 Source is unchanged by acquisition.	not checked
Analysis:	Expected results achieved

5.2.14　DA-06-FW

Test Case DA-06-FW X-Ways 14.8	
Case Summary:	DA-06 Acquire a physical device using access interface AI to an image file.
Assertions:	AM-01 The tool uses access interface SRC-AI to access the digital source. AM-02 The tool acquires digital source DS. AM-03 The tool executes in execution environment XE. AM-05 If image file creation is specified, the tool creates an image file on file system type FS. AM-06 All visible sectors are acquired from the digital source. AM-08 All sectors acquired from the digital source are acquired accurately. AO-01 If the tool creates an image file, the data represented by the image file is the same as the data acquired by the tool. AO-05 If the tool creates a multi-file image of a requested size then all the individual files shall be no larger than the requested size. AO-22 If requested, the tool calculates block hashes for a specified block size during an acquisition for each block acquired from the digital source. AO-23 If the tool logs any log significant information, the information is accurately recorded in the log file. AO-24 If the tool executes in a forensically safe execution environment, the digital source is unchanged by the acquisition process.
Tester Name:	mrmw
Test Host:	Joe
Test Date:	Mon Jul 28 14:23:27 2008
Drives:	src(01-IDE) dst (none) other (05-FU)
Source Setup:	src hash (SHA1): < A48BB5665D6DC57C22DB68E2F723DA9AA8DF82B9 > src hash (MD5): < F458F673894753FA6A0EC8B8EC63848E > 78165360 total sectors (40020664320 bytes) Model (0BB-00JHC0) serial # (WD-WMAMC74171) N Start LBA Length Start C/H/S End C/H/S boot Partition type 1 P 000000063 020980827 0000/001/01 1023/254/63 0C Fat32X 2 X 020980890 057175335 1023/000/01 1023/254/63 0F extended 3 S 000000063 000032067 1023/001/01 1023/254/63 01 Fat12 4 x 000032130 002104515 1023/000/01 1023/254/63 05 extended 5 S 000000063 002104452 1023/001/01 1023/254/63 06 Fat16 6 x 002136645 004192965 1023/000/01 1023/254/63 05 extended 7 S 000000063 004192902 1023/001/01 1023/254/63 16 other 8 x 006329610 008401995 1023/000/01 1023/254/63 05 extended 9 S 000000063 008401932 1023/001/01 1023/254/63 0B Fat32 10 x 014731605 010490445 1023/000/01 1023/254/63 05 extended 11 S 000000063 010490382 1023/001/01 1023/254/63 83 Linux 12 x 025222050 004209030 1023/000/01 1023/254/63 05 extended 13 S 000000063 004208967 1023/001/01 1023/254/63 82 Linux swap 14 x 029431080 027744255 1023/000/01 1023/254/63 05 extended 15 S 000000063 027744192 1023/001/01 1023/254/63 07 NTFS 16 S 000000000 000000000 0000/000/00 0000/000/00 00 empty entry 17 P 000000000 000000000 0000/000/00 0000/000/00 00 empty entry 18 P 000000000 000000000 0000/000/00 0000/000/00 00 empty entry 1 020980827 sectors 10742183424 bytes 3 000032067 sectors 16418304 bytes 5 002104452 sectors 1077479424 bytes 7 004192902 sectors 2146765824 bytes 9 008401932 sectors 4301789184 bytes 11 010490382 sectors 5371075584 bytes 13 004208967 sectors 2154991104 bytes 15 027744192 sectors 14205026304 bytes
Log Highlights:	====== Tool Settings: ====== size CD (640MB) hash sha1 verify no Write Block: 32 Tableau T5 OS: Microsoft Windows 2000 [Version 5.00.2195]

Test Case DA-06-FW X-Ways 14.8

```
====== Extract from X-Ways log.txt file ======
Model: WDC WD400BB-00JHC0      05.0
Total capacity: 40,020,664,320 bytes = 37.3 GB
Sector count: 78,165,360
Hash of source data: A48BB5665D6DC57C22DB68E2F723DA9AA8DF82B9 (SHA-1)
```

Results:

Assertion & Expected Result	Actual Result
AM-01 Source acquired using interface AI.	as expected
AM-02 Source is type DS.	as expected
AM-03 Execution environment is XE.	as expected
AM-05 An image is created on file system type FS.	as expected
AM-06 All visible sectors acquired.	as expected
AM-08 All sectors accurately acquired.	as expected
AO-01 Image file is complete and accurate.	as expected
AO-05 Multifile image created.	as expected
AO-22 Tool calculates hashes by block.	option not available
AO-23 Logged information is correct.	as expected
AO-24 Source is unchanged by acquisition.	not checked

Analysis: Expected results achieved

5.2.15　DA-06-ATA28

Test Case DA-06-ATA28 X-Ways 14.8	
Case Summary:	DA-06 Acquire a physical device using access interface AI to an image file.
Assertions:	AM-01 The tool uses access interface SRC-AI to access the digital source. AM-02 The tool acquires digital source DS. AM-03 The tool executes in execution environment XE. AM-05 If image file creation is specified, the tool creates an image file on file system type FS. AM-06 All visible sectors are acquired from the digital source. AM-08 All sectors acquired from the digital source are acquired accurately. AO-01 If the tool creates an image file, the data represented by the image file is the same as the data acquired by the tool. AO-05 If the tool creates a multi-file image of a requested size then all the individual files shall be no larger than the requested size. AO-22 If requested, the tool calculates block hashes for a specified block size during an acquisition for each block acquired from the digital source. AO-23 If the tool logs any log significant information, the information is accurately recorded in the log file. AO-24 If the tool executes in a forensically safe execution environment, the digital source is unchanged by the acquisition process.
Tester Name:	mrmw
Test Host:	Freddy
Test Date:	Mon Jun 30 12:03:30 2008
Drives:	src(43) dst (none) other (01-FU)
Source Setup:	src hash (SHA256): < 2658F47603DE6B1D883B64823E9733F578658D08D06A4BB8C053C4F57BDC615E > src hash (SHA1): < 888E2E7F7AD237DC7A732281DD93F325065E5871 > src hash (MD5): < BC39C3F7EE7A50E77B9BA1E65A5AEEF7 > 78125000 total sectors (40000000000 bytes) Model (0BB-75JHC0　　　) serial # (　　　WD-WMAMC46588)<pre>N Start LBA Length Start C/H/S End C/H/S boot Partition type
1 P 000000063 020980827 0000/001/01 1023/254/63   0C Fat32X
2 X 020980890 057143205 1023/000/01 1023/254/63   0F extended
3 S 000000063 000032067 1023/001/01 1023/254/63   01 Fat12
4 x 000032130 002104515 1023/000/01 1023/254/63   05 extended
5 S 000000063 002104452 1023/001/01 1023/254/63   06 Fat16
6 x 002136645 004192965 1023/000/01 1023/254/63   05 extended
7 S 000000063 004192902 1023/001/01 1023/254/63   16 other
8 x 006329610 008401995 1023/000/01 1023/254/63   05 extended
9 S 000000063 008401932 1023/001/01 1023/254/63   0B Fat32
10 x 014731605 010490445 1023/000/01 1023/254/63   05 extended
11 S 000000063 010490382 1023/001/01 1023/254/63   83 Linux
12 x 025222050 004209030 1023/000/01 1023/254/63   05 extended
13 S 000000063 004208967 1023/001/01 1023/254/63   82 Linux swap
14 x 029431080 027712125 1023/000/01 1023/254/63   05 extended
15 S 000000063 027712062 1023/001/01 1023/254/63   07 NTFS
16 S 000000000 000000000 0000/000/00 0000/000/00   00 empty entry
17 P 000000000 000000000 0000/000/00 0000/000/00   00 empty entry
18 P 000000000 000000000 0000/000/00 0000/000/00   00 empty entry
1 020980827 sectors 10742183424 bytes
3 000032067 sectors 16418304 bytes
5 002104452 sectors 1077479424 bytes
7 004192902 sectors 2146765824 bytes
9 008401932 sectors 4301789184 bytes
11 010490382 sectors 5371075584 bytes
13 004208967 sectors 2154991104 bytes
15 027712062 sectors 14188575744 bytes</pre>
Log Highlights:	====== Tool Settings: ====== size CD hash md5sum verify no Write Block: 19 MyKey Technology NoWrite

Test Case DA-06-ATA28 X-Ways 14.8

OS: Microsoft Windows 2000 [Version 5.00.2195]

====== Extract from X-Ways log.txt file ======
Model: WDC WD400BB-75JHC0
Total capacity: 40,000,000,000 bytes = 37.3 GB
Sector count: 78,125,000
Hash of source data: BC39C3F7EE7A50E77B9BA1E65A5AEEF7 (MD5)

Results:

Assertion & Expected Result	Actual Result
AM-01 Source acquired using interface AI.	as expected
AM-02 Source is type DS.	as expected
AM-03 Execution environment is XE.	as expected
AM-05 An image is created on file system type FS.	as expected
AM-06 All visible sectors acquired.	as expected
AM-08 All sectors accurately acquired.	as expected
AO-01 Image file is complete and accurate.	as expected
AO-05 Multifile image created.	as expected
AO-22 Tool calculates hashes by block.	option not available
AO-23 Logged information is correct.	as expected
AO-24 Source is unchanged by acquisition.	not checked

Analysis: Expected results achieved

5.2.16　　DA-06-ATA48

Test Case DA-06-ATA48 X-Ways 14.8	
Case Summary:	DA-06 Acquire a physical device using access interface AI to an image file.
Assertions:	AM-01 The tool uses access interface SRC-AI to access the digital source. AM-02 The tool acquires digital source DS. AM-03 The tool executes in execution environment XE. AM-05 If image file creation is specified, the tool creates an image file on file system type FS. AM-06 All visible sectors are acquired from the digital source. AM-08 All sectors acquired from the digital source are acquired accurately. AO-01 If the tool creates an image file, the data represented by the image file is the same as the data acquired by the tool. AO-05 If the tool creates a multi-file image of a requested size then all the individual files shall be no larger than the requested size. AO-22 If requested, the tool calculates block hashes for a specified block size during an acquisition for each block acquired from the digital source. AO-23 If the tool logs any log significant information, the information is accurately recorded in the log file. AO-24 If the tool executes in a forensically safe execution environment, the digital source is unchanged by the acquisition process.
Tester Name:	mrmw
Test Host:	Frank
Test Date:	Mon Jun 30 13:02:54 2008
Drives:	src(4C) dst (none) other (06-FU)
Source Setup:	src hash (SHA1): < 8FF620D2BEDCCAFE8412EDAAD56C8554F872EFBF > src hash (MD5): < D10F763B56D4CEBA2D1311C61F9FB382 > 390721968 total sectors (200049647616 bytes) 24320/254/63 (max cyl/hd values) 24321/255/63 (number of cyl/hd) IDE disk: Model (WDC WD2000JB-00KFA0) serial # (WD-WMAMR1031111) N Start LBA Length Start C/H/S End C/H/S boot Partition type 1 P 000000063 390700737 0000/001/01 1023/254/63 Boot 07 NTFS 2 P 000000000 000000000 0000/000/00 0000/000/00 00 empty entry 3 P 000000000 000000000 0000/000/00 0000/000/00 00 empty entry 4 P 000000000 000000000 0000/000/00 0000/000/00 00 empty entry 1 390700737 sectors 200038777344 bytes
Log Highlights:	====== Tool Settings: ====== size 2000MB hash sha-1 verify yes Write Block: 3 Intelligent Computer Solutions FastBloc IDE OS: Microsoft Windows XP [Version 5.1.2600] ====== Extract from X-Ways log.txt file ====== Model: WDC WD2000JB-00KFA0 Total capacity: 200,049,647,616 bytes = 186 GB Sector count: 390,721,968 Hash of source data: 8FF620D2BEDCCAFE8412EDAAD56C8554F872EFBF (SHA-1)
Results:	

Assertion & Expected Result	Actual Result
AM-01 Source acquired using interface AI.	as expected
AM-02 Source is type DS.	as expected
AM-03 Execution environment is XE.	as expected
AM-05 An image is created on file system type FS.	as expected
AM-06 All visible sectors acquired.	as expected
AM-08 All sectors accurately acquired.	as expected
AO-01 Image file is complete and accurate.	as expected
AO-05 Multifile image created.	as expected
AO-22 Tool calculates hashes by block.	option not available
AO-23 Logged information is correct.	as expected

Test Case DA-06-ATA48 X-Ways 14.8		
	AO-24 Source is unchanged by acquisition.	not checked
Analysis:	Expected results achieved	

5.2.17   DA-06-CF

Test Case DA-06-CF X-Ways 14.8	
Case Summary:	DA-06 Acquire a physical device using access interface AI to an image file.
Assertions:	AM-01 The tool uses access interface SRC-AI to access the digital source. AM-02 The tool acquires digital source DS. AM-03 The tool executes in execution environment XE. AM-05 If image file creation is specified, the tool creates an image file on file system type FS. AM-06 All visible sectors are acquired from the digital source. AM-08 All sectors acquired from the digital source are acquired accurately. AO-01 If the tool creates an image file, the data represented by the image file is the same as the data acquired by the tool. AO-05 If the tool creates a multi-file image of a requested size then all the individual files shall be no larger than the requested size. AO-22 If requested, the tool calculates block hashes for a specified block size during an acquisition for each block acquired from the digital source. AO-23 If the tool logs any log significant information, the information is accurately recorded in the log file. AO-24 If the tool executes in a forensically safe execution environment, the digital source is unchanged by the acquisition process.
Tester Name:	mrmw
Test Host:	Frank
Test Date:	Tue Jul 1 11:41:06 2008
Drives:	src(C1-CF) dst (none) other (01-FU)
Source Setup:	src hash (SHA256): < C7CF0218222DF80D5316511D6814266C7FA507C13F795AD3D323BB73C1590D80 > src hash (SHA1): < 5B8235178DF99FA307430C088F81746606638A0B > src hash (MD5): < 776DF8B4D2589E21DEBCF589EDC16D78 > 503808 total sectors (257949696 bytes)
Log Highlights:	====== Tool Settings: ====== size 2000MB hash sha1 verify yes Write Block: 7 Digital Intelligence UltraBlock Forensic Card Reader ====== Extract from X-Ways log.txt file ====== Model: ICSI CF Card CF Total capacity: 257,949,696 bytes = 246 MB Sector count: 503,808 Hash of source data: 5B8235178DF99FA307430C088F81746606638A0B (SHA-1)
Results:	

Assertion & Expected Result	Actual Result
AM-01 Source acquired using interface AI.	as expected
AM-02 Source is type DS.	as expected
AM-03 Execution environment is XE.	as expected
AM-05 An image is created on file system type FS.	as expected
AM-06 All visible sectors acquired.	as expected
AM-08 All sectors accurately acquired.	as expected
AO-01 Image file is complete and accurate.	as expected
AO-05 Multifile image created.	as expected
AO-22 Tool calculates hashes by block.	option not available
AO-23 Logged information is correct.	as expected
AO-24 Source is unchanged by acquisition.	not checked

Analysis:	Expected results achieved

5.2.18   DA-06-FLOPPY

Test Case DA-06-FLOPPY X-Ways 14.8	
Case Summary:	DA-06 Acquire a physical device using access interface AI to an image file.
Assertions:	AM-01 The tool uses access interface SRC-AI to access the digital source. AM-02 The tool acquires digital source DS. AM-03 The tool executes in execution environment XE. AM-05 If image file creation is specified, the tool creates an image file on file system type FS. AM-06 All visible sectors are acquired from the digital source. AM-08 All sectors acquired from the digital source are acquired accurately. AO-01 If the tool creates an image file, the data represented by the image file is the same as the data acquired by the tool. AO-05 If the tool creates a multi-file image of a requested size then all the individual files shall be no larger than the requested size. AO-22 If requested, the tool calculates block hashes for a specified block size during an acquisition for each block acquired from the digital source. AO-23 If the tool logs any log significant information, the information is accurately recorded in the log file. AO-24 If the tool executes in a forensically safe execution environment, the digital source is unchanged by the acquisition process.
Tester Name:	mrmw
Test Host:	Frank
Test Date:	Wed Jun 25 09:12:45 2008
Drives:	src(floppy) dst (none) other (01-FU)
Source Setup:	src hash (SHA1): < e2863334ac7eaabc7c8a0d62eb0d3b3af29f2c40 > src hash (MD5): < 17f6a5925be2f38eedaf435ff8b6a6f4 > Floppy disk
Log Highlights:	====== Tool Settings: ====== size CD hash md5sum verify yes OS: Microsoft Windows XP [Version 5.1.2600] ====== Extract from X-Ways log.txt file ====== Model: ? Total capacity: 1,474,560 bytes = 1.4 MB Sector count: 2,880 Hash of source data: 17F6A5925BE2F38EEDAF435FF8B6A6F4 (MD5)
Results:	

Assertion & Expected Result	Actual Result
AM-01 Source acquired using interface AI.	as expected
AM-02 Source is type DS.	as expected
AM-03 Execution environment is XE.	as expected
AM-05 An image is created on file system type FS.	as expected
AM-06 All visible sectors acquired.	as expected
AM-08 All sectors accurately acquired.	as expected
AO-01 Image file is complete and accurate.	as expected
AO-05 Multifile image created.	as expected
AO-22 Tool calculates hashes by block.	option not available
AO-23 Logged information is correct.	as expected
AO-24 Source is unchanged by acquisition.	not checked

Analysis:	Expected results achieved

5.2.19   DA-06-PART

Test Case DA-06-PART X-Ways 14.8	
Case Summary:	DA-06 Acquire a physical device using access interface AI to an image file.
Assertions:	AM-01 The tool uses access interface SRC-AI to access the digital source. AM-02 The tool acquires digital source DS. AM-03 The tool executes in execution environment XE. AM-05 If image file creation is specified, the tool creates an image file on file system type FS. AM-06 All visible sectors are acquired from the digital source. AM-08 All sectors acquired from the digital source are acquired accurately. AO-01 If the tool creates an image file, the data represented by the image file is the same as the data acquired by the tool. AO-05 If the tool creates a multi-file image of a requested size then all the individual files shall be no larger than the requested size. AO-22 If requested, the tool calculates block hashes for a specified block size during an acquisition for each block acquired from the digital source. AO-23 If the tool logs any log significant information, the information is accurately recorded in the log file. AO-24 If the tool executes in a forensically safe execution environment, the digital source is unchanged by the acquisition process.
Tester Name:	mrmw
Test Host:	Freddy
Test Date:	Mon Aug 4 23:56:59 2008
Drives:	src(24-FU2) dst (none) other (05-FU)
Source Setup:	src hash (SHA1): < A78EDB5E90298D0CDF199B4B62119F81208A252A > src hash (MD5): < 90311DDF672B8CBA0869A46F4A455A7E > 39070080 total sectors (20003880960 bytes) 19076/063/32 (max cyl/hd values) 19077/064/32 (number of cyl/hd) Model (ATCS04-0) serial # (CSH206D9DSEL) Reference SHA1 Hash of first 7,814,016 sectors for 24-FU2 [root (knoppix)]# dd count=7814016 bs=512 if=/dev/sda | sha1sum 7814016+0 records in 7814016+0 records out 4000776192 bytes (4.0 GB) copied, 458.05 seconds, 8.7 MB/s 745d4481b477f92fc8c85ba3e63f28d0013aca36 - [root (knoppix)]#
Log Highlights:	====== Tool Settings: ====== size default (2047 MB) hash sha1 verify no Write Block: 18 Tableay Forensic USB Bridge OS: Microsoft Windows XP [Version 5.1.2600] ====== Extract from X-Ways log.txt file ====== Model: IC25N020ATCS04-0 Total capacity: 20,003,880,960 bytes = 18.6 GB Sector count: 39,070,080 Hash of source data: 745D4481B477F92FC8C85BA3E63F28D0013ACA36 (SHA-1)
Results:	

Assertion & Expected Result	Actual Result
AM-01 Source acquired using interface AI.	as expected
AM-02 Source is type DS.	as expected
AM-03 Execution environment is XE.	as expected
AM-05 An image is created on file system type FS.	as expected
AM-06 All visible sectors acquired.	as expected
AM-08 All sectors accurately acquired.	as expected
AO-01 Image file is complete and accurate.	as expected
AO-05 Multifile image created.	as expected

Test Case DA-06-PART X-Ways 14.8		
	AO-22 Tool calculates hashes by block.	option not available
	AO-23 Logged information is correct.	as expected
	AO-24 Source is unchanged by acquisition.	not checked
Analysis:	Expected results achieved	

5.2.20 DA-06-SATA28

Test Case DA-06-SATA28 X-Ways 14.8	
Case Summary:	DA-06 Acquire a physical device using access interface AI to an image file.
Assertions:	AM-01 The tool uses access interface SRC-AI to access the digital source. AM-02 The tool acquires digital source DS. AM-03 The tool executes in execution environment XE. AM-05 If image file creation is specified, the tool creates an image file on file system type FS. AM-06 All visible sectors are acquired from the digital source. AM-08 All sectors acquired from the digital source are acquired accurately. AO-01 If the tool creates an image file, the data represented by the image file is the same as the data acquired by the tool. AO-05 If the tool creates a multi-file image of a requested size then all the individual files shall be no larger than the requested size. AO-22 If requested, the tool calculates block hashes for a specified block size during an acquisition for each block acquired from the digital source. AO-23 If the tool logs any log significant information, the information is accurately recorded in the log file. AO-24 If the tool executes in a forensically safe execution environment, the digital source is unchanged by the acquisition process.
Tester Name:	brl
Test Host:	Freddy
Test Date:	Mon Feb 14 13:42:52 2011
Drives:	src(01-SATA) dst (none) other (3E-SATA)
Source Setup:	src hash (SHA256): < 1AA01FEAE55F5CD55185D2B1A1359B3F913E7093FEF1D1ADA220CAC456BA40D8 > src hash (SHA1): < 4951236428C36B944E62E8D65862DCBEF05F282C > src hash (MD5): < 0A49B13D91FA9DA87CEEE9D006CB6FD6 > 156301488 total sectors (80026361856 bytes) Model (0JD-32HKA0) serial # (WD-WMAJ91448529)
Log Highlights:	====== Tool Settings: ====== size 2000MB hash sha-1 verify no Write Block: none OS: Microsoft Windows XP [Version 5.1.2600] ====== Extract from X-Ways log.txt file ====== Model: WDC WD800JD-32HKA0 Total capacity: 80,026,361,856 bytes = 74.5 GB Sector count: 156,301,488 Sector count: 156,301,488 [according to ATA] Hash of source data: 4951236428C36B944E62E8D65862DCBEF05F282C (SHA-1)
Results:	

Assertion & Expected Result	Actual Result
AM-01 Source acquired using interface AI.	as expected
AM-02 Source is type DS.	as expected
AM-03 Execution environment is XE.	as expected
AM-05 An image is created on file system type FS.	as expected
AM-06 All visible sectors acquired.	as expected
AM-08 All sectors accurately acquired.	as expected
AO-01 Image file is complete and accurate.	as expected
AO-05 Multifile image created.	as expected
AO-22 Tool calculates hashes by block.	option not available
AO-23 Logged information is correct.	as expected
AO-24 Source is unchanged by acquisition.	as expected

Test Case DA-06-SATA28 X-Ways 14.8	
Analysis:	Expected results achieved

5.2.21   DA-06-SATA48

Test Case DA-06-SATA48 X-Ways 14.8	
Case Summary:	DA-06 Acquire a physical device using access interface AI to an image file.
Assertions:	AM-01 The tool uses access interface SRC-AI to access the digital source. AM-02 The tool acquires digital source DS. AM-03 The tool executes in execution environment XE. AM-05 If image file creation is specified, the tool creates an image file on file system type FS. AM-06 All visible sectors are acquired from the digital source. AM-08 All sectors acquired from the digital source are acquired accurately. AO-01 If the tool creates an image file, the data represented by the image file is the same as the data acquired by the tool. AO-05 If the tool creates a multi-file image of a requested size then all the individual files shall be no larger than the requested size. AO-22 If requested, the tool calculates block hashes for a specified block size during an acquisition for each block acquired from the digital source. AO-23 If the tool logs any log significant information, the information is accurately recorded in the log file. AO-24 If the tool executes in a forensically safe execution environment, the digital source is unchanged by the acquisition process.
Tester Name:	brl
Test Host:	Freddy
Test Date:	Mon Feb 14 16:26:48 2011
Drives:	src(0B-SATA) dst (none) other (3E-SATA)
Source Setup:	src hash (SHA1): < DA892EE968DD828F2F1B6825C1D3EF35062A0737 > src hash (MD5): < 1873847F597A69D0F5DB991B67E84F92 > 488397168 total sectors (250059350016 bytes) 30400/254/63 (max cyl/hd values) 30401/255/63 (number of cyl/hd) Model (00JD-22FYB0) serial # (WD-WMAEH2677545)
Log Highlights:	====== Tool Settings: ====== size 2000MB hash sha-1 verify no Write Block: none OS: Microsoft Windows XP [Version 5.1.2600] ====== Extract from X-Ways log.txt file ====== Model: WDC WD2500JD-22FYB0 Total capacity: 250,059,350,016 bytes = 233 GB Sector count: 488,397,168 Sector count: 488,397,168 [according to ATA] Hash of source data: DA892EE968DD828F2F1B6825C1D3EF35062A0737 (SHA-1)

Results:		
	Assertion & Expected Result	**Actual Result**
	AM-01 Source acquired using interface AI.	as expected
	AM-02 Source is type DS.	as expected
	AM-03 Execution environment is XE.	as expected
	AM-05 An image is created on file system type FS.	as expected
	AM-06 All visible sectors acquired.	as expected
	AM-08 All sectors accurately acquired.	as expected
	AO-01 Image file is complete and accurate.	as expected
	AO-05 Multifile image created.	as expected
	AO-22 Tool calculates hashes by block.	option not available
	AO-23 Logged information is correct.	as expected
	AO-24 Source is unchanged by acquisition.	as expected

Analysis:	Expected results achieved

5.2.22 DA-06-SCSI

Test Case DA-06-SCSI X-Ways 14.8	
Case Summary:	DA-06 Acquire a physical device using access interface AI to an image file.
Assertions:	AM-01 The tool uses access interface SRC-AI to access the digital source. AM-02 The tool acquires digital source DS. AM-03 The tool executes in execution environment XE. AM-05 If image file creation is specified, the tool creates an image file on file system type FS. AM-06 All visible sectors are acquired from the digital source. AM-08 All sectors acquired from the digital source are acquired accurately. AO-01 If the tool creates an image file, the data represented by the image file is the same as the data acquired by the tool. AO-05 If the tool creates a multi-file image of a requested size then all the individual files shall be no larger than the requested size. AO-22 If requested, the tool calculates block hashes for a specified block size during an acquisition for each block acquired from the digital source. AO-23 If the tool logs any log significant information, the information is accurately recorded in the log file. AO-24 If the tool executes in a forensically safe execution environment, the digital source is unchanged by the acquisition process.
Tester Name:	mrmw
Test Host:	Frank
Test Date:	Tue Jul 29 09:16:34 2008
Drives:	src(E0) dst (none) other (FU-01)
Source Setup:	src hash (SHA1): < 4A6941F1337A8A22B10FC844B4D7FA6158BECB82 > src hash (MD5): < A97C8F36B7AC9D5233B90AC09284F938 > 17938985 total sectors (9184760320 bytes) Model (ATLAS10K2-TY092J) serial # (169028142436)
Log Highlights:	====== Tool Settings: ====== size 2047 MB hash sha1 verify no OS: Microsoft Windows [Version 5.2.3790] ====== Extract from X-Ways log.txt file ====== Model: QUANTUM ATLAS10K2-TY092J Total capacity: 9,184,760,320 bytes = 8.6 GB Sector count: 17,938,985 Hash of source data: 4A6941F1337A8A22B10FC844B4D7FA6158BECB82 (SHA-1)

Results:	Assertion & Expected Result	Actual Result
	AM-01 Source acquired using interface AI.	as expected
	AM-02 Source is type DS.	as expected
	AM-03 Execution environment is XE.	as expected
	AM-05 An image is created on file system type FS.	as expected
	AM-06 All visible sectors acquired.	as expected
	AM-08 All sectors accurately acquired.	as expected
	AO-01 Image file is complete and accurate.	as expected
	AO-05 Multifile image created.	as expected
	AO-22 Tool calculates hashes by block.	option not available
	AO-23 Logged information is correct.	as expected
	AO-24 Source is unchanged by acquisition.	not checked
Analysis:	Expected results achieved

5.2.23 DA-06-USB

Case Summary:	DA-06 Acquire a physical device using access interface AI to an image file.
Assertions:	AM-01 The tool uses access interface SRC-AI to access the digital source. AM-02 The tool acquires digital source DS. AM-03 The tool executes in execution environment XE. AM-05 If image file creation is specified, the tool creates an image file on file system type FS. AM-06 All visible sectors are acquired from the digital source. AM-08 All sectors acquired from the digital source are acquired accurately. AO-01 If the tool creates an image file, the data represented by the image file is the same as the data acquired by the tool. AO-05 If the tool creates a multi-file image of a requested size then all the individual files shall be no larger than the requested size. AO-22 If requested, the tool calculates block hashes for a specified block size during an acquisition for each block acquired from the digital source. AO-23 If the tool logs any log significant information, the information is accurately recorded in the log file. AO-24 If the tool executes in a forensically safe execution environment, the digital source is unchanged by the acquisition process.
Tester Name:	mrmw
Test Host:	Freddy
Test Date:	Mon Aug 4 09:21:20 2008
Drives:	src(63-FU2) dst (none) other (05-FU)
Source Setup:	src hash (SHA256): < EC8EF011494BA6DA18F74C47547C3E74E7180585096A830F9247A98EF613BB1D > src hash (SHA1): < F7069EDCBEAC863C88DECED82159F22DA96BE99B > src hash (MD5): < EE217BC4FA4F3D1B4021D29B065AA9EC > 117304992 total sectors (60060155904 bytes) Model (SP0612N) serial # () N Start LBA Length Start C/H/S End C/H/S boot Partition type 1 P 000000063 004192902 0000/001/01 0260/254/63 Boot 06 Fat16 2 X 004192965 113097600 0261/000/01 1023/254/63 0F extended 3 S 000000063 113097537 0261/001/01 1023/254/63 0B Fat32 4 S 000000000 000000000 0000/000/00 0000/000/00 00 empty entry 5 P 000000000 000000000 0000/000/00 0000/000/00 00 empty entry 6 P 000000000 000000000 0000/000/00 0000/000/00 00 empty entry 1 004192902 sectors 2146765824 bytes 3 113097537 sectors 57905938944 bytes
Log Highlights:	====== Tool Settings: ====== size CD (640 MB) hash md5sum verify no Write Block: 18 Tableau Forensic USB Bridge OS: Microsoft Windows XP [Version 5.1.2600] ====== Extract from X-Ways log.txt file ====== Model: SAMSUNG SP0612N Total capacity: 60,060,155,904 bytes = 55.9 GB Sector count: 117,304,992 Hash of source data: EE217BC4FA4F3D1B4021D29B065AA9EC (MD5)
Results:	(table below)

Assertion & Expected Result	Actual Result
AM-01 Source acquired using interface AI.	as expected
AM-02 Source is type DS.	as expected
AM-03 Execution environment is XE.	as expected
AM-05 An image is created on file system type FS.	as expected
AM-06 All visible sectors acquired.	as expected
AM-08 All sectors accurately acquired.	as expected
AO-01 Image file is complete and accurate.	as expected

Test Case DA-06-USB X-Ways 14.8		
	AO-05 Multifile image created.	as expected
	AO-22 Tool calculates hashes by block.	option not available
	AO-23 Logged information is correct.	as expected
	AO-24 Source is unchanged by acquisition.	not checked
Analysis:	Expected results achieved	

5.2.24 DA-07-F12

Test Case DA-07-F12 X-Ways 14.8	
Case Summary:	DA-07 Acquire a digital source of type DS to an image file.
Assertions:	AM-01 The tool uses access interface SRC-AI to access the digital source. AM-02 The tool acquires digital source DS. AM-03 The tool executes in execution environment XE. AM-05 If image file creation is specified, the tool creates an image file on file system type FS. AM-06 All visible sectors are acquired from the digital source. AM-08 All sectors acquired from the digital source are acquired accurately. AO-01 If the tool creates an image file, the data represented by the image file is the same as the data acquired by the tool. AO-05 If the tool creates a multi-file image of a requested size then all the individual files shall be no larger than the requested size. AO-22 If requested, the tool calculates block hashes for a specified block size during an acquisition for each block acquired from the digital source. AO-23 If the tool logs any log significant information, the information is accurately recorded in the log file. AO-24 If the tool executes in a forensically safe execution environment, the digital source is unchanged by the acquisition process.
Tester Name:	mrmw
Test Host:	Frank
Test Date:	Fri Jul 25 09:38:07 2008
Drives:	src(01-IDE) dst (none) other (06-FU)
Source Setup:	src hash (SHA1): < A48BB5665D6DC57C22DB68E2F723DA9AA8DF82B9 > src hash (MD5): < F458F673894753FA6A0EC8B8EC63848E > 78165360 total sectors (40020664320 bytes) Model (0BB-00JHC0) serial # (WD-WMAMC74171) <pre> N Start LBA Length Start C/H/S End C/H/S boot Partition type 1 P 000000063 020980827 0000/001/01 1023/254/63 0C Fat32X 2 X 020980890 057175335 1023/000/01 1023/254/63 0F extended 3 S 000000063 000032067 1023/001/01 1023/254/63 01 Fat12 4 x 000032130 002104515 1023/000/01 1023/254/63 05 extended 5 S 000000063 002104452 1023/001/01 1023/254/63 06 Fat16 6 x 002136645 004192965 1023/000/01 1023/254/63 05 extended 7 S 000000063 004192902 1023/001/01 1023/254/63 16 other 8 x 006329610 008401995 1023/000/01 1023/254/63 05 extended 9 S 000000063 008401932 1023/001/01 1023/254/63 0B Fat32 10 x 014731605 010490445 1023/000/01 1023/254/63 05 extended 11 S 000000063 010490382 1023/001/01 1023/254/63 83 Linux 12 x 025222050 004209030 1023/000/01 1023/254/63 05 extended 13 S 000000063 004208967 1023/001/01 1023/254/63 82 Linux swap 14 x 029431080 027744255 1023/000/01 1023/254/63 05 extended 15 S 000000063 027744192 1023/001/01 1023/254/63 07 NTFS 16 S 000000000 000000000 0000/000/00 0000/000/00 00 empty entry 17 P 000000000 000000000 0000/000/00 0000/000/00 00 empty entry 18 P 000000000 000000000 0000/000/00 0000/000/00 00 empty entry 1 020980827 sectors 10742183424 bytes 3 000032067 sectors 16418304 bytes 5 002104452 sectors 1077479424 bytes 7 004192902 sectors 2146765824 bytes 9 008401932 sectors 4301789184 bytes 11 010490382 sectors 5371075584 bytes 13 004208967 sectors 2154991104 bytes 15 027744192 sectors 14205026304 bytes 01F12-md5 16418303 E20E3CFEA80BF6F2D2AA75E829CC8CD9 01F12-sha1 16418303 F8B72B65436DE3BD394ACFF71D405D0389C0E9B7</pre>
Log Highlights:	====== Tool Settings: ====== default (2047 MB) Write Block: 32 Tableau T5 OS: Microsoft Windows [Version 5.2.3790]

Test Case DA-07-F12 X-Ways 14.8	
	====== Extract from X-Ways log.txt file ====== Total capacity: 16,418,304 bytes = 15.7 MB Hash of source data: E20E3CFEA80BF6F2D2AA75E829CC8CD9 (MD5)
Results:	

Assertion & Expected Result	Actual Result
AM-01 Source acquired using interface AI.	as expected
AM-02 Source is type DS.	as expected
AM-03 Execution environment is XE.	as expected
AM-05 An image is created on file system type FS.	as expected
AM-06 All visible sectors acquired.	as expected
AM-08 All sectors accurately acquired.	as expected
AO-01 Image file is complete and accurate.	as expected
AO-05 Multifile image created.	as expected
AO-22 Tool calculates hashes by block.	option not available
AO-23 Logged information is correct.	as expected
AO-24 Source is unchanged by acquisition.	not checked

Analysis:	Expected results achieved

5.2.25   DA-07-F16

Test Case DA-07-F16 X-Ways 14.8	
Case Summary:	DA-07 Acquire a digital source of type DS to an image file.
Assertions:	AM-01 The tool uses access interface SRC-AI to access the digital source. AM-02 The tool acquires digital source DS. AM-03 The tool executes in execution environment XE. AM-05 If image file creation is specified, the tool creates an image file on file system type FS. AM-06 All visible sectors are acquired from the digital source. AM-08 All sectors acquired from the digital source are acquired accurately. AO-01 If the tool creates an image file, the data represented by the image file is the same as the data acquired by the tool. AO-05 If the tool creates a multi-file image of a requested size then all the individual files shall be no larger than the requested size. AO-22 If requested, the tool calculates block hashes for a specified block size during an acquisition for each block acquired from the digital source. AO-23 If the tool logs any log significant information, the information is accurately recorded in the log file. AO-24 If the tool executes in a forensically safe execution environment, the digital source is unchanged by the acquisition process.
Tester Name:	mw
Test Host:	Freddy
Test Date:	Wed Jul 9 11:40:33 2008
Drives:	src(43) dst (01-FU) other (none)
Source Setup:	src hash (SHA256): < 2658F47603DE6B1D883B64823E9733F578658D08D06A4BB8C053C4F57BDC615E > src hash (SHA1): < 888E2E7F7AD237DC7A732281DD93F325065E5871 > src hash (MD5): < BC39C3F7EE7A50E77B9BA1E65A5AEEF7 > 78125000 total sectors (40000000000 bytes) Model (0BB-75JHC0) serial # (WD-WMAMC46588)<pre>N Start LBA Length Start C/H/S End C/H/S boot Partition type
1 P 000000063 020980827 0000/001/01 1023/254/63   0C Fat32X
2 X 020980890 057143205 1023/000/01 1023/254/63   0F extended
3 S 000000063 000032067 1023/001/01 1023/254/63   01 Fat12
4 x 000032130 002104515 1023/000/01 1023/254/63   05 extended
5 S 000000063 002104452 1023/001/01 1023/254/63   06 Fat16
6 x 002136645 004192965 1023/000/01 1023/254/63   05 extended
7 S 000000063 004192902 1023/001/01 1023/254/63   16 other
8 x 006329610 008401995 1023/000/01 1023/254/63   05 extended
9 S 000000063 008401932 1023/001/01 1023/254/63   0B Fat32
10 x 014731605 010490445 1023/000/01 1023/254/63   05 extended
11 S 000000063 010490382 1023/001/01 1023/254/63   83 Linux
12 x 025222050 004209030 1023/000/01 1023/254/63   05 extended
13 S 000000063 004208967 1023/001/01 1023/254/63   82 Linux swap
14 x 029431080 027712125 1023/000/01 1023/254/63   05 extended
15 S 000000063 027712062 1023/001/01 1023/254/63   07 NTFS
16 S 000000000 000000000 0000/000/00 0000/000/00   00 empty entry
17 P 000000000 000000000 0000/000/00 0000/000/00   00 empty entry
18 P 000000000 000000000 0000/000/00 0000/000/00   00 empty entry
1 020980827 sectors 10742183424 bytes
3 000032067 sectors 16418304 bytes
5 002104452 sectors 1077479424 bytes
7 004192902 sectors 2146765824 bytes
9 008401932 sectors 4301789184 bytes
11 010490382 sectors 5371075584 bytes
13 004208967 sectors 2154991104 bytes
15 027712062 sectors 14188575744 bytes</pre>43F16-md5sum 1077479423 37E81FFB31C3CB38AA48B2237500908E 43F16-sha1sum 1077479423 443CCEC9A22F726DAF6CE384817151C83B3EBC8B
Log Highlights:	====== Tool Settings: ====== size CD hash sha-1 verify no

Test Case DA-07-F16 X-Ways 14.8	
	Write Block: 32 Tableau T5 OS: Microsoft Windows XP [Version 5.1.2600] ====== Extract from X-Ways log.txt file ====== Total capacity: 1,077,479,424 bytes = 1.0 GB Hash of source data: 443CCEC9A22F726DAF6CE384817151C83B3EBC8B (SHA-1)
Results:	

Assertion & Expected Result	Actual Result
AM-01 Source acquired using interface AI.	as expected
AM-02 Source is type DS.	as expected
AM-03 Execution environment is XE.	as expected
AM-05 An image is created on file system type FS.	as expected
AM-06 All visible sectors acquired.	as expected
AM-08 All sectors accurately acquired.	as expected
AO-01 Image file is complete and accurate.	as expected
AO-05 Multifile image created.	as expected
AO-22 Tool calculates hashes by block.	option not available
AO-23 Logged information is correct.	as expected
AO-24 Source is unchanged by acquisition.	not checked

Analysis:	Expected results achieved

5.2.26   DA-07-F32

Test Case DA-07-F32 X-Ways 14.8	
Case Summary:	DA-07 Acquire a digital source of type DS to an image file.
Assertions:	AM-01 The tool uses access interface SRC-AI to access the digital source. AM-02 The tool acquires digital source DS. AM-03 The tool executes in execution environment XE. AM-05 If image file creation is specified, the tool creates an image file on file system type FS. AM-06 All visible sectors are acquired from the digital source. AM-08 All sectors acquired from the digital source are acquired accurately. AO-01 If the tool creates an image file, the data represented by the image file is the same as the data acquired by the tool. AO-05 If the tool creates a multi-file image of a requested size then all the individual files shall be no larger than the requested size. AO-22 If requested, the tool calculates block hashes for a specified block size during an acquisition for each block acquired from the digital source. AO-23 If the tool logs any log significant information, the information is accurately recorded in the log file. AO-24 If the tool executes in a forensically safe execution environment, the digital source is unchanged by the acquisition process.
Tester Name:	mrmw
Test Host:	Frank
Test Date:	Fri Jul 18 12:44:54 2008
Drives:	src(01-IDE) dst (none) other (06-FU)

Source Setup:	src hash (SHA1): < A48BB5665D6DC57C22DB68E2F723DA9AA8DF82B9 >
	src hash (MD5): < F458F673894753FA6A0EC8B8EC63848E >
	78165360 total sectors (40020664320 bytes)
	Model (0BB-00JHC0) serial # (WD-WMAMC74171)
	<pre>N Start LBA Length Start C/H/S End C/H/S boot Partition type
	 1 P 000000063 020980827 0000/001/01 1023/254/63 0C Fat32X
	 2 X 020980890 057175335 1023/000/01 1023/254/63 0F extended
	 3 S 000000063 000032067 1023/001/01 1023/254/63 01 Fat12
	 4 x 000032130 002104515 1023/000/01 1023/254/63 05 extended
	 5 S 000000063 002104452 1023/001/01 1023/254/63 06 Fat16
	 6 x 002136645 004192965 1023/000/01 1023/254/63 05 extended
	 7 S 000000063 004192902 1023/001/01 1023/254/63 16 other
	 8 x 006329610 008401995 1023/000/01 1023/254/63 05 extended
	 9 S 000000063 008401932 1023/001/01 1023/254/63 0B Fat32
	10 x 014731605 010490445 1023/000/01 1023/254/63 05 extended
	11 S 000000063 010490382 1023/001/01 1023/254/63 83 Linux
	12 x 025222050 004209030 1023/000/01 1023/254/63 05 extended
	13 S 000000063 004208967 1023/001/01 1023/254/63 82 Linux swap
	14 x 029431080 027744255 1023/000/01 1023/254/63 05 extended
	15 S 000000063 027744192 1023/001/01 1023/254/63 07 NTFS
	16 S 000000000 000000000 0000/000/00 0000/000/00 00 empty entry
	17 P 000000000 000000000 0000/000/00 0000/000/00 00 empty entry
	18 P 000000000 000000000 0000/000/00 0000/000/00 00 empty entry
	 1 020980827 sectors 10742183424 bytes
	 3 000032067 sectors 16418304 bytes
	 5 002104452 sectors 1077479424 bytes
	 7 004192902 sectors 2146765824 bytes
	 9 008401932 sectors 4301789184 bytes
	11 010490382 sectors 5371075584 bytes
	13 004208967 sectors 2154991104 bytes
	15 027744192 sectors 14205026304 bytes
	01F32-md5 4301789183 BFF7DC64C54339DA2A9D7972C076B514
	01F32-sha1 4301789183 B861D9E999F39750B484FFB693FF69DEC090C6B8</pre>

Log Highlights:	====== Tool Settings: ====== size CD hash md5 verify no Write Block: 32 Tableau T5

Test Case DA-07-F32 X-Ways 14.8	
	OS: Microsoft Windows 2000 [Version 5.00.2195] ====== Extract from X-Ways log.txt file ====== Total capacity: 4,301,789,184 bytes = 4.0 GB Hash of source data: BFF7DC64C54339DA2A9D7972C076B514 (MD5)

Results:

Assertion & Expected Result	Actual Result
AM-01 Source acquired using interface AI.	as expected
AM-02 Source is type DS.	as expected
AM-03 Execution environment is XE.	as expected
AM-05 An image is created on file system type FS.	as expected
AM-06 All visible sectors acquired.	as expected
AM-08 All sectors accurately acquired.	as expected
AO-01 Image file is complete and accurate.	as expected
AO-05 Multifile image created.	as expected
AO-22 Tool calculates hashes by block.	option not available
AO-23 Logged information is correct.	as expected
AO-24 Source is unchanged by acquisition.	not checked

Analysis: Expected results achieved

5.2.27　　DA-07-F32X

Test Case DA-07-F32X X-Ways 14.8	
Case Summary:	DA-07 Acquire a digital source of type DS to an image file.
Assertions:	AM-01 The tool uses access interface SRC-AI to access the digital source. AM-02 The tool acquires digital source DS. AM-03 The tool executes in execution environment XE. AM-05 If image file creation is specified, the tool creates an image file on file system type FS. AM-06 All visible sectors are acquired from the digital source. AM-08 All sectors acquired from the digital source are acquired accurately. AO-01 If the tool creates an image file, the data represented by the image file is the same as the data acquired by the tool. AO-05 If the tool creates a multi-file image of a requested size then all the individual files shall be no larger than the requested size. AO-22 If requested, the tool calculates block hashes for a specified block size during an acquisition for each block acquired from the digital source. AO-23 If the tool logs any log significant information, the information is accurately recorded in the log file. AO-24 If the tool executes in a forensically safe execution environment, the digital source is unchanged by the acquisition process.
Tester Name:	mrmw
Test Host:	Frank
Test Date:	Fri Jul 25 13:09:00 2008
Drives:	src(43) dst (none) other (01-FU)

Source Setup:	src hash (SHA256): <
	2658F47603DE6B1D883B64823E9733F578658D08D06A4BB8C053C4F57BDC615E >
	src hash (SHA1): < 888E2E7F7AD237DC7A732281DD93F325065E5871 >
	src hash (MD5): < BC39C3F7EE7A50E77B9BA1E65A5AEEF7 >
	78125000 total sectors (40000000000 bytes)
	Model (0BB-75JHC0) serial # (WD-WMAMC46588)
	<pre>N Start LBA Length Start C/H/S End C/H/S boot Partition type
	 1 P 000000063 020980827 0000/001/01 1023/254/63 0C Fat32X
	 2 X 020980890 057143205 1023/000/01 1023/254/63 0F extended
	 3 S 000000063 000032067 1023/001/01 1023/254/63 01 Fat12
	 4 x 000032130 002104515 1023/000/01 1023/254/63 05 extended
	 5 S 000000063 002104452 1023/001/01 1023/254/63 06 Fat16
	 6 x 002136645 004192965 1023/000/01 1023/254/63 05 extended
	 7 S 000000063 004192902 1023/001/01 1023/254/63 16 other
	 8 x 006329610 008401995 1023/000/01 1023/254/63 05 extended
	 9 S 000000063 008401932 1023/001/01 1023/254/63 0B Fat32
	10 x 014731605 010490445 1023/000/01 1023/254/63 05 extended
	11 S 000000063 010490382 1023/001/01 1023/254/63 83 Linux
	12 x 025222050 004209030 1023/000/01 1023/254/63 05 extended
	13 S 000000063 004208967 1023/001/01 1023/254/63 82 Linux swap
	14 x 029431080 027712125 1023/000/01 1023/254/63 05 extended
	15 S 000000063 027712062 1023/001/01 1023/254/63 07 NTFS
	16 S 000000000 000000000 0000/000/00 0000/000/00 00 empty entry
	17 P 000000000 000000000 0000/000/00 0000/000/00 00 empty entry
	18 P 000000000 000000000 0000/000/00 0000/000/00 00 empty entry
	 1 020980827 sectors 10742183424 bytes
	 3 000032067 sectors 16418304 bytes
	 5 002104452 sectors 1077479424 bytes
	 7 004192902 sectors 2146765824 bytes
	 9 008401932 sectors 4301789184 bytes
	11 010490382 sectors 5371075584 bytes
	13 004208967 sectors 2154991104 bytes
	15 027712062 sectors 14188575744 bytes</pre>43F32x-md5sum 10742183424 5980CB0FA68E9862C65765DF50F00906
	43F32x-sha1sum 10742183423 379C1AC47AF956FC8C80389C2A7427A7F8FB4E89

Log Highlights:	====== Tool Settings: ====== size default (2047 MB) hash sha1 verify no

```
Test Case DA-07-F32X X-Ways 14.8
```

	Write Block: 32 Tableau T5 OS: Microsoft Windows [Version 5.2.3790] ====== Extract from X-Ways log.txt file ====== Total capacity: 10,742,183,424 bytes = 10.0 GB Hash of source data: 379C1AC47AF956FC8C80389C2A7427A7F8FB4E89 (SHA-1)

Results:

Assertion & Expected Result	Actual Result
AM-01 Source acquired using interface AI.	as expected
AM-02 Source is type DS.	as expected
AM-03 Execution environment is XE.	as expected
AM-05 An image is created on file system type FS.	as expected
AM-06 All visible sectors acquired.	as expected
AM-08 All sectors accurately acquired.	as expected
AO-01 Image file is complete and accurate.	as expected
AO-05 Multifile image created.	as expected
AO-22 Tool calculates hashes by block.	option not available
AO-23 Logged information is correct.	as expected
AO-24 Source is unchanged by acquisition.	not checked

Analysis: Expected results achieved

5.2.28   DA-07-NTFS

Test Case DA-07-NTFS X-Ways 14.8	
Case Summary:	DA-07 Acquire a digital source of type DS to an image file.
Assertions:	AM-01 The tool uses access interface SRC-AI to access the digital source. AM-02 The tool acquires digital source DS. AM-03 The tool executes in execution environment XE. AM-05 If image file creation is specified, the tool creates an image file on file system type FS. AM-06 All visible sectors are acquired from the digital source. AM-08 All sectors acquired from the digital source are acquired accurately. AO-01 If the tool creates an image file, the data represented by the image file is the same as the data acquired by the tool. AO-05 If the tool creates a multi-file image of a requested size then all the individual files shall be no larger than the requested size. AO-22 If requested, the tool calculates block hashes for a specified block size during an acquisition for each block acquired from the digital source. AO-23 If the tool logs any log significant information, the information is accurately recorded in the log file. AO-24 If the tool executes in a forensically safe execution environment, the digital source is unchanged by the acquisition process.
Tester Name:	mrmw
Test Host:	Frank
Test Date:	Thu Jul 17 14:16:11 2008
Drives:	src(01-IDE) dst (none) other (06-FU)

Source Setup:	src hash (SHA1): < A48BB5665D6DC57C22DB68E2F723DA9AA8DF82B9 >
	src hash (MD5): < F458F673894753FA6A0EC8B8EC63848E >
	78165360 total sectors (40020664320 bytes)
	Model (0BB-00JHC0) serial # (WD-WMAMC74171)
	  N Start LBA Length Start C/H/S End C/H/S boot Partition type
	  1 P 000000063 020980827 0000/001/01 1023/254/63 0C Fat32X
	  2 X 020980890 057175335 1023/000/01 1023/254/63 0F extended
	  3 S 000000063 000032067 1023/001/01 1023/254/63 01 Fat12
	  4 x 000032130 002104515 1023/000/01 1023/254/63 05 extended
	  5 S 000000063 002104452 1023/001/01 1023/254/63 06 Fat16
	  6 x 002136645 004192965 1023/000/01 1023/254/63 05 extended
	  7 S 000000063 004192902 1023/001/01 1023/254/63 16 other
	  8 x 006329610 008401995 1023/000/01 1023/254/63 05 extended
	  9 S 000000063 008401932 1023/001/01 1023/254/63 0B Fat32
	10 x 014731605 010490445 1023/000/01 1023/254/63 05 extended
	11 S 000000063 010490382 1023/001/01 1023/254/63 83 Linux
	12 x 025222050 004209030 1023/000/01 1023/254/63 05 extended
	13 S 000000063 004208967 1023/001/01 1023/254/63 82 Linux swap
	14 x 029431080 027744255 1023/000/01 1023/254/63 05 extended
	15 S 000000063 027744192 1023/001/01 1023/254/63 07 NTFS
	16 S 000000000 000000000 0000/000/00 0000/000/00 00 empty entry
	17 P 000000000 000000000 0000/000/00 0000/000/00 00 empty entry
	18 P 000000000 000000000 0000/000/00 0000/000/00 00 empty entry
	 1 020980827 sectors 10742183424 bytes
	 3 000032067 sectors 16418304 bytes
	 5 002104452 sectors 1077479424 bytes
	 7 004192902 sectors 2146765824 bytes
	 9 008401932 sectors 4301789184 bytes
	11 010490382 sectors 5371075584 bytes
	13 004208967 sectors 2154991104 bytes
	15 027744192 sectors 14205026304 bytes
	01NTFS-md5 14205026303 92B27B30BEE8B0FFBA8C660FA1590D49
	01NTFS-sha1 14205026303 0FBA4C36295CB9622CD815577429C3A588C34D09
	01NTFS-sha256 14205026303
	65FCD168163625E5EB74255B2A981B6F1C9D6259AF8A0851369101986A7ABC09

Log Highlights:	====== Tool Settings: ====== size cd Write Block: 32 Tableau T5

Test Case DA-07-NTFS X-Ways 14.8	
	OS: Microsoft Windows XP [Version 5.1.2600] ====== Extract from X-Ways log.txt file ====== Total capacity: 14,205,022,208 bytes = 13.2 GB Hash of source data: 28A3A4330007F75B8AFA99D38FFCD257 (MD5)

Results:

Assertion & Expected Result	Actual Result
AM-01 Source acquired using interface AI.	as expected
AM-02 Source is type DS.	as expected
AM-03 Execution environment is XE.	as expected
AM-05 An image is created on file system type FS.	as expected
AM-06 All visible sectors acquired.	last 8 sectors not acquired
AM-08 All sectors accurately acquired.	as expected
AO-01 Image file is complete and accurate.	as expected
AO-05 Multifile image created.	as expected
AO-22 Tool calculates hashes by block.	option not available
AO-23 Logged information is correct.	as expected
AO-24 Source is unchanged by acquisition.	not checked

Analysis:	Expected results not achieved

5.2.29 DA-07-THUMB

Test Case DA-07-THUMB X-Ways 14.8	
Case Summary:	DA-07 Acquire a digital source of type DS to an image file.
Assertions:	AM-01 The tool uses access interface SRC-AI to access the digital source. AM-02 The tool acquires digital source DS. AM-03 The tool executes in execution environment XE. AM-05 If image file creation is specified, the tool creates an image file on file system type FS. AM-06 All visible sectors are acquired from the digital source. AM-08 All sectors acquired from the digital source are acquired accurately. AO-01 If the tool creates an image file, the data represented by the image file is the same as the data acquired by the tool. AO-05 If the tool creates a multi-file image of a requested size then all the individual files shall be no larger than the requested size. AO-22 If requested, the tool calculates block hashes for a specified block size during an acquisition for each block acquired from the digital source. AO-23 If the tool logs any log significant information, the information is accurately recorded in the log file. AO-24 If the tool executes in a forensically safe execution environment, the digital source is unchanged by the acquisition process.
Tester Name:	brl
Test Host:	Freddy
Test Date:	Fri Feb 11 10:41:28 2011
Drives:	src(D5-THUMB) dst (none) other (3E-SATA)
Source Setup:	src hash (SHA1): < D68520EF74A336E49DCCF83815B7B08FDC53E38A > src hash (MD5): < C843593624B2B3B878596D8760B19954 > 505856 total sectors (258998272 bytes) Model (usb2.0Flash Disk) serial # ()
Log Highlights:	====== Tool Settings: ====== size FAT (2000 MB) hash SHA1 Write Block: 18 Tableau Forensic USB Bridge OS: Microsoft Windows XP [Version 5.1.2600] ====== Extract from X-Ways log.txt file ====== Total capacity: 258,998,272 bytes = 247 MB Hash of source data: D68520EF74A336E49DCCF83815B7B08FDC53E38A (SHA-1)
Results:	

Assertion & Expected Result	Actual Result
AM-01 Source acquired using interface AI.	as expected
AM-02 Source is type DS.	as expected
AM-03 Execution environment is XE.	as expected
AM-05 An image is created on file system type FS.	as expected
AM-06 All visible sectors acquired.	as expected
AM-08 All sectors accurately acquired.	as expected
AO-01 Image file is complete and accurate.	as expected
AO-05 Multifile image created.	as expected
AO-22 Tool calculates hashes by block.	option not available
AO-23 Logged information is correct.	as expected
AO-24 Source is unchanged by acquisition.	not checked

Analysis:	Expected results achieved

5.2.30 DA-08-ATA28

Case Summary:	DA-08 Acquire a physical drive with hidden sectors to an image file.
Assertions:	AM-01 The tool uses access interface SRC-AI to access the digital source. AM-02 The tool acquires digital source DS. AM-03 The tool executes in execution environment XE. AM-05 If image file creation is specified, the tool creates an image file on file system type FS. AM-06 All visible sectors are acquired from the digital source. AM-07 All hidden sectors are acquired from the digital source. AM-08 All sectors acquired from the digital source are acquired accurately. AO-01 If the tool creates an image file, the data represented by the image file is the same as the data acquired by the tool. AO-05 If the tool creates a multi-file image of a requested size then all the individual files shall be no larger than the requested size. AO-22 If requested, the tool calculates block hashes for a specified block size during an acquisition for each block acquired from the digital source. AO-23 If the tool logs any log significant information, the information is accurately recorded in the log file. AO-24 If the tool executes in a forensically safe execution environment, the digital source is unchanged by the acquisition process.
Tester Name:	mrmw
Test Host:	Frank
Test Date:	Wed Aug 27 15:08:23 2008
Drives:	src(7E) dst (none) other (05-FU)
Source Setup:	src hash (SHA1): < 60A77A87F1FA085B1808A88B19F6B36AECE52381 > src hash (MD5): < 62F17D0DF3EB0562E008A736154F71CF > 78177792 total sectors (40027029504 bytes) 65534/015/63 (max cyl/hd values) 65535/016/63 (number of cyl/hd) IDE disk: Model (MAXTOR 6L040J2) serial # (662201136780) HPA created Hashes with HPA in place Maximum Addressable Sector: 70,000,000 sha1: CC0CFFDE461D774228370DBAD1E4BD5C8413C346
Log Highlights:	====== Tool Settings: ====== size default (2074 MB) Write Block: none OS: Microsoft Windows [Version 5.2.3790] ====== Extract from X-Ways log.txt file ====== Model: MAXTOR 6L040J2 Total capacity: 35,840,000,512 bytes = 33.4 GB Sector count: 70,000,001 Sector count: ? [according to ATA] Hash of source data: CC0CFFDE461D774228370DBAD1E4BD5C8413C346 (SHA-1)

Results:

Assertion & Expected Result	Actual Result
AM-01 Source acquired using interface AI.	as expected
AM-02 Source is type DS.	as expected
AM-03 Execution environment is XE.	as expected
AM-05 An image is created on file system type FS.	as expected
AM-06 All visible sectors acquired.	as expected
AM-07 All hidden sectors acquired.	HPA not acquired
AM-08 All sectors accurately acquired.	as expected
AO-01 Image file is complete and accurate.	as expected
AO-05 Multifile image created.	as expected
AO-22 Tool calculates hashes by block.	option not available

Test Case DA-08-ATA28 X-Ways 14.8		
	AO-23 Logged information is correct.	as expected
	AO-24 Source is unchanged by acquisition.	not checked
Analysis:	Expected results not achieved	

5.2.31　　DA-08-ATA48

Test Case DA-08-ATA48 X-Ways 14.8	
Case Summary:	DA-08 Acquire a physical drive with hidden sectors to an image file.
Assertions:	AM-01 The tool uses access interface SRC-AI to access the digital source. AM-02 The tool acquires digital source DS. AM-03 The tool executes in execution environment XE. AM-05 If image file creation is specified, the tool creates an image file on file system type FS. AM-06 All visible sectors are acquired from the digital source. AM-07 All hidden sectors are acquired from the digital source. AM-08 All sectors acquired from the digital source are acquired accurately. AO-01 If the tool creates an image file, the data represented by the image file is the same as the data acquired by the tool. AO-05 If the tool creates a multi-file image of a requested size then all the individual files shall be no larger than the requested size. AO-22 If requested, the tool calculates block hashes for a specified block size during an acquisition for each block acquired from the digital source. AO-23 If the tool logs any log significant information, the information is accurately recorded in the log file. AO-24 If the tool executes in a forensically safe execution environment, the digital source is unchanged by the acquisition process.
Tester Name:	mrmw
Test Host:	Joe
Test Date:	Wed Aug 27 15:34:30 2008
Drives:	src(2D-IDE) dst (none) other (01-FU)
Source Setup:	src hash (SHA1): < 1B30BF7A8B2F27FFAEDE461A7FC4A2B3E53FB56A > src hash (MD5): < B7E8F9BFC5ABEEA446BF7616D65EDE3C > 490234752 total sectors (251000193024 bytes) 30514/254/63 (max cyl/hd values) 30515/255/63 (number of cyl/hd) IDE disk: Model (Maxtor 7Y250P0) serial # (Y63C6YTE) HPA created Hashes with HPA in place for 2D-IDE Maximum Addressable Sector: 440,000,000 MD5: D6790082B29ABC10C9D2F0B9559D42B3
Log Highlights:	====== Tool Settings: ====== size CD (640 MB) Write Block: none OS: Microsoft Windows XP [Version 5.1.2600] ====== Extract from X-Ways log.txt file ====== Model: Maxtor 7Y250P0 Total capacity: 225,280,000,512 bytes = 210 GB Sector count: 440,000,001 Sector count: 490,234,752 [according to ATA] !!! Hash of source data: D6790082B29ABC10C9D2F0B9559D42B3 (MD5)
Results:	

Assertion & Expected Result	Actual Result
AM-01 Source acquired using interface AI.	as expected
AM-02 Source is type DS.	as expected
AM-03 Execution environment is XE.	as expected
AM-05 An image is created on file system type FS.	as expected
AM-06 All visible sectors acquired.	as expected
AM-07 All hidden sectors acquired.	HPA not acquired
AM-08 All sectors accurately acquired.	as expected
AO-01 Image file is complete and accurate.	as expected
AO-05 Multifile image created.	as expected
AO-22 Tool calculates hashes by block.	option not available

Test Case DA-08-ATA48 X-Ways 14.8		
	AO-23 Logged information is correct.	as expected
	AO-24 Source is unchanged by acquisition.	not checked
Analysis:	Expected results not achieved	

5.2.32   DA-08-DCO

Test Case DA-08-DCO X-Ways 14.8	
Case Summary:	DA-08 Acquire a physical drive with hidden sectors to an image file.
Assertions:	AM-01 The tool uses access interface SRC-AI to access the digital source. AM-02 The tool acquires digital source DS. AM-03 The tool executes in execution environment XE. AM-05 If image file creation is specified, the tool creates an image file on file system type FS. AM-06 All visible sectors are acquired from the digital source. AM-07 All hidden sectors are acquired from the digital source. AM-08 All sectors acquired from the digital source are acquired accurately. AO-01 If the tool creates an image file, the data represented by the image file is the same as the data acquired by the tool. AO-05 If the tool creates a multi-file image of a requested size then all the individual files shall be no larger than the requested size. AO-22 If requested, the tool calculates block hashes for a specified block size during an acquisition for each block acquired from the digital source. AO-23 If the tool logs any log significant information, the information is accurately recorded in the log file. AO-24 If the tool executes in a forensically safe execution environment, the digital source is unchanged by the acquisition process.
Tester Name:	mrme
Test Host:	Frank
Test Date:	Wed Aug 27 13:14:01 2008
Drives:	src(51-IDE) dst (none) other (05-FU)
Source Setup:	src hash (SHA1): < B9186B6373E5D4C15706D624FF8D3029F4E49C3D > src hash (MD5): < 28B8DD3FDA3392823C5F6596B9AB3A80 > 312581808 total sectors (160041885696 bytes) 19456/254/63 (max cyl/hd values) 19457/255/63 (number of cyl/hd) IDE disk: Model (WDC WD1600JB-00GVC0) serial # (WD-WMAL94887547) Hashes with HPA in place for 2D-IDE Maximum Addressable Sector: 270,000,000 MD5: A7DA2CF45B122C972BE42E4F454F583D
Log Highlights:	====== Tool Settings: ====== FAT (2000MB) Write Block: none OS: Microsoft Windows 2000 [Version 5.00.2195] ====== Extract from X-Ways log.txt file ====== Model: WDC WD1600JB-00GVC0 Total capacity: 137,438,952,960 bytes = 128 GB Sector count: 268,435,455 Sector count: 312,581,808 [according to ATA] !!! Hash of source data: FA25F1768BDD01441ED6628F84B89C4A (MD5)
Results:	

Assertion & Expected Result	Actual Result
AM-01 Source acquired using interface AI.	as expected
AM-02 Source is type DS.	as expected
AM-03 Execution environment is XE.	as expected
AM-05 An image is created on file system type FS.	as expected
AM-06 All visible sectors acquired.	48-bit address sectors skipped
AM-07 All hidden sectors acquired.	DCO not acquired
AM-08 All sectors accurately acquired.	as expected
AO-01 Image file is complete and accurate.	as expected
AO-05 Multifile image created.	as expected
AO-22 Tool calculates hashes by block.	option not available

	AO-23 Logged information is correct.	as expected
	AO-24 Source is unchanged by acquisition.	not checked
Analysis:	Expected results not achieved	

5.2.33　DA-09-ATA

Test Case DA-09-ATA X-Ways 14.8	
Case Summary:	DA-09 Acquire a digital source that has at least one faulty data sector.
Assertions:	AM-01 The tool uses access interface SRC-AI to access the digital source. AM-02 The tool acquires digital source DS. AM-03 The tool executes in execution environment XE. AM-05 If image file creation is specified, the tool creates an image file on file system type FS. AM-06 All visible sectors are acquired from the digital source. AM-08 All sectors acquired from the digital source are acquired accurately. AM-09 If unresolved errors occur while reading from the selected digital source, the tool notifies the user of the error type and location within the digital source. AM-10 If unresolved errors occur while reading from the selected digital source, the tool uses a benign fill in the destination object in place of the inaccessible data. AO-01 If the tool creates an image file, the data represented by the image file is the same as the data acquired by the tool. AO-05 If the tool creates a multi-file image of a requested size then all the individual files shall be no larger than the requested size. AO-22 If requested, the tool calculates block hashes for a specified block size during an acquisition for each block acquired from the digital source. AO-23 If the tool logs any log significant information, the information is accurately recorded in the log file. AO-24 If the tool executes in a forensically safe execution environment, the digital source is unchanged by the acquisition process.
Tester Name:	mrmw
Test Host:	Joe
Test Date:	Tue Aug 5 07:38:57 2008
Drives:	src(CPR1) dst (23-IDE) other (none)
Source Setup:	No before hash for CPR1 　120103200 total sectors (61492838400 bytes) 　Drive with known bad sectors 　Vendor: Maxtor　Model: DiamondMax Plus 9 Known Bad Sector List for ED-CPR-BAD-1 Manufacturer: Maxtor Model: 6Y060L0 DiamondMax Plus 9 Serial Number: Y27KR6CE Capacity: 60GB Interface: PATA 54 faulty sectors 10069095, 10069911, 12023808, 18652594, 18656041, 18656857, 18660303, 18661119, 19746716-19746717, 22233904, 23098370, 23383001, 24102466- 24102467, 24104250, 24106656, 24107458, 28959971-28959972, 41825791, 41828995, 52654580, 52655318, 60522984, 68643842-68643843, 69973290, 72714626, 72715293, 82148809, 82148810, 83810525, 85310861, 85313430, 85314038-85314039, 86321211, 86323780, 87186066, 87856313, 87856922, 97191260-97191261, 100093150-100093151, 103861021, 109706975-109706976, 110347947, 110350122-110350123, 115664758, 115835518
Log Highlights:	====== Destination drive setup ====== 195813072 sectors wiped with 23 ====== Comparison of original to clone drive ====== Sectors compared: 120103200 Sectors match:　　120103146 Sectors differ:　　　　54 Bytes differ:　　　27640 Diffs range 10069095, 10069911, 12023808, 18652594, 18656041, 18656857, 18660303, 18661119, 19746716-19746717, 22233904, 23098370, 23383001, 24102466-24102467, 24104250, 24106656, 24107458, 28959971-28959972, 41825791, 41828995,

```
52654580, 52655318, 60522984, 68643842-68643843, 69973290,
72714626, 72715293, 82148809-82148810, 83810525, 85310861,
85313430, 85314038-85314039, 86321211, 86323780, 87186066,
87856313, 87856922, 97191260-97191261, 100093150-100093151,
103861021, 109706975-109706976, 110347947, 110350122-110350123,
115664758, 115835518
Source (120103200) has 75709872 fewer sectors than destination (195813072)
Zero fill:                    0
Src Byte fill (ED):           0
Dst Byte fill (23): 75709872
Other fill:                   0
Other no fill:                0
Zero fill range:
Src fill range:
Dst fill range:   120103200-195813071
Other fill range:
Other not filled range:
0 source read errors, 0 destination read errors


====== Tool Settings: ======
fill ? BAD SECTOR ?
avoid no
skip NA
simult no

OS: Microsoft Windows [Version 5.2.3790]

====== Extract from X-Ways log.txt file ======
Sectors that could not be read:
10,069,095
10,069,911
12,023,808
18,652,594
18,656,041
     . . .
110,347,947
110,350,122
110,350,123
115,664,758
115,835,518

08/05/2008, 10:40:37.3
120,103,146 sector(s) successfully copied.
54 bad source sectors encountered.
Corresponding destination sectors filled with:   ? BAD SECTOR ?
====== Summary of Sectors not acquired ======
2 different run lengths observed in 44 runs
34 runs of length 1
10 runs of length 2
54 sectors differ
     0 zero filled and 1 varying non-zero filled
```

	Assertion & Expected Result	Actual Result
Results:		
	AM-01 Source acquired using interface AI.	as expected
	AM-02 Source is type DS.	as expected
	AM-03 Execution environment is XE.	as expected
	AM-05 An image is created on file system type FS.	as expected
	AM-06 All visible sectors acquired.	as expected
	AM-08 All sectors accurately acquired.	as expected
	AM-09 Error logged.	as expected
	AM-10 Benign fill replaces inaccessible sectors.	as expected
	AO-01 Image file is complete and accurate.	as expected
	AO-05 Multifile image created.	as expected
	AO-22 Tool calculates hashes by block.	option not available
	AO-23 Logged information is correct.	as expected
	AO-24 Source is unchanged by acquisition.	not checked

Test Case DA-09-ATA X-Ways 14.8	
Analysis:	Expected results achieved

5.2.34   DA-09-FW

Test Case DA-09-FW X-Ways 14.8	
Case Summary:	DA-09 Acquire a digital source that has at least one faulty data sector.
Assertions:	AM-01 The tool uses access interface SRC-AI to access the digital source. AM-02 The tool acquires digital source DS. AM-03 The tool executes in execution environment XE. AM-05 If image file creation is specified, the tool creates an image file on file system type FS. AM-06 All visible sectors are acquired from the digital source. AM-08 All sectors acquired from the digital source are acquired accurately. AM-09 If unresolved errors occur while reading from the selected digital source, the tool notifies the user of the error type and location within the digital source. AM-10 If unresolved errors occur while reading from the selected digital source, the tool uses a benign fill in the destination object in place of the inaccessible data. AO-01 If the tool creates an image file, the data represented by the image file is the same as the data acquired by the tool. AO-05 If the tool creates a multi-file image of a requested size then all the individual files shall be no larger than the requested size. AO-22 If requested, the tool calculates block hashes for a specified block size during an acquisition for each block acquired from the digital source. AO-23 If the tool logs any log significant information, the information is accurately recorded in the log file. AO-24 If the tool executes in a forensically safe execution environment, the digital source is unchanged by the acquisition process.
Tester Name:	mrmw
Test Host:	Joe
Test Date:	Wed Aug 6 14:59:43 2008
Drives:	src(ED-BAD-CPR1) dst (23-IDE) other (none)

Source Setup:	No before hash for ED-BAD-CPR1
	  120103200 total sectors (61492838400 bytes)
	  Drive with known bad sectors
	  Vendor: Maxtor Model: DiamondMax Plus 9
	
	Known Bad Sector List for ED-CPR-BAD-1
	
	Manufacturer: Maxtor
	Model: 6Y060L0 DiamondMax Plus 9
	Serial Number: Y27KR6CE
	Capacity: 60GB
	Interface: PATA
	
	54 faulty sectors
	10069095, 10069911, 12023808, 18652594, 18656041, 18656857, 18660303,
	18661119, 19746716-19746717, 22233904, 23098370, 23383001, 24102466-
	24102467, 24104250, 24106656, 24107458, 28959971-28959972, 41825791,
	41828995, 52654580, 52655318, 60522984, 68643842-68643843, 69973290,
	72714626, 72715293, 82148809, 82148810, 83810525, 85310861, 85313430,
	85314038-85314039, 86321211, 86323780, 87186066, 87856313, 87856922,
	97191260-97191261, 100093150-100093151, 103861021, 109706975-109706976,
	110347947, 110350122-110350123, 115664758, 115835518

Log Highlights:	====== Destination drive setup ====== 195813072 sectors wiped with 23 ====== Comparison of original to clone drive ====== Sectors compared: 120103200 Sectors match: 119992852 Sectors differ: 110348 Bytes differ: 2886952 Diffs range 10068736-10072567, 10072824-10073087, 12022528-12026359, 12026616-12026879, 18648832-18652663, 18652920-18653183, 18653440-18657271, 18657528-18657791, 18658048-18661879, 18662136-18662399, 19745536-19749367, 19749624-19749887,

```
                22233856-22237687, 22237944-22238207, 23095552-23099383,
                23099640-23099903, 23381248-23385079, 23385336-23385599,
                24100096-24103927, 24104184-24104447, 24104704-24108535,
                24108792-24109055, 28956928-28960759, 28961016-28961279,
                41822464-41826295, 41826552-41826815, 41827072-41830903,
                41831160-41831423, 52654580-52654581, 52655318-52655319,
                60521728-60525559, 60525816-60526079, 68641024-68644855,
                68645112-68645375, 69972736-69976567, 69976824-69977087,
                72714496-72718327, 82147072-82150903, 82151160-82151423,
                83810525-83810526, 85308160-85311991, 85312248-85312511,
                85312768-85316599, 85316856-85317119, 86321211-86321212,
                86321920-86325751, 86326008-86326271, 87183616-87187447,
                87187704-87187967, 87856313-87856314, 87856922-87856923,
                97187584-97191415, 97191672-97191935, 100090624-100094455,
                100094712-100094975, 103859968-103863799, 103864056-103864319,
                109706975-109706976, 110347947-110347948, 110350122-110350123,
                115661056-115664887, 115665144-115665407, 115835518-115835519
                Source (120103200) has 75709872 fewer sectors than destination (195813072)
                Zero fill:             0
                Src Byte fill (ED):    0
                Dst Byte fill (23): 75709872
                Other fill:            0
                Other no fill:         0
                Zero fill range:
                Src fill range:
                Dst fill range:  120103200-195813071
                Other fill range:
                Other not filled range:
                0 source read errors, 0 destination read errors


                ====== Tool Settings: ======
                avoid yes
                write 1
                write ? BAD SECTOR ?
                simuly yes

                Write Block: 32 Tableau Forensic IDE Bridge

                OS: Microsoft Windows 2000 [Version 5.00.2195]

                ====== Extract from X-Ways log.txt file ======
                Sectors that could not be read:
                52,654,580
                52,654,581..52,654,581 skipped.
                52,655,318
                52,655,319..52,655,319 skipped.
                83,810,525
                    . . .
                110,350,122
                110,350,123..110,350,123 skipped.
                115,835,518
                115,835,519..115,835,519 skipped.

                08/07/2008, 08:30:22.5
                120,103,180 sector(s) successfully copied.
                10 skipped. (Requested skip range was 1 sectors.)
                10 bad source sectors encountered.
                Corresponding destination sectors filled with:  ? BAD SECTOR ?
                ====== Summary of Sectors not acquired ======
                3 different run lengths observed in 63 runs
                10 runs of length 2
                26 runs of length 264
                27 runs of length 3832
                110348 sectors differ
                    0 zero filled and 12 varying non-zero filled
```

Results:		
	Assertion & Expected Result	**Actual Result**
	AM-01 Source acquired using interface AI.	as expected

Test Case DA-09-FW X-Ways 14.8		
	AM-02 Source is type DS.	as expected
	AM-03 Execution environment is XE.	as expected
	AM-05 An image is created on file system type FS.	as expected
	AM-06 All visible sectors acquired.	some sectors skipped
	AM-08 All sectors accurately acquired.	as expected
	AM-09 Error logged.	as expected
	AM-10 Benign fill replaces inaccessible sectors.	as expected
	AO-01 Image file is complete and accurate.	as expected
	AO-05 Multifile image created.	as expected
	AO-22 Tool calculates hashes by block.	option not available
	AO-23 Logged information is correct.	as expected
	AO-24 Source is unchanged by acquisition.	not checked
Analysis:	Expected results not achieved	

5.2.35 DA-09-FW-XP

Test Case DA-09-FW-XP X-Ways 14.8	
Case Summary:	DA-09 Acquire a digital source that has at least one faulty data sector.
Assertions:	AM-01 The tool uses access interface SRC-AI to access the digital source. AM-02 The tool acquires digital source DS. AM-03 The tool executes in execution environment XE. AM-05 If image file creation is specified, the tool creates an image file on file system type FS. AM-06 All visible sectors are acquired from the digital source. AM-08 All sectors acquired from the digital source are acquired accurately. AM-09 If unresolved errors occur while reading from the selected digital source, the tool notifies the user of the error type and location within the digital source. AM-10 If unresolved errors occur while reading from the selected digital source, the tool uses a benign fill in the destination object in place of the inaccessible data. AO-01 If the tool creates an image file, the data represented by the image file is the same as the data acquired by the tool. AO-05 If the tool creates a multi-file image of a requested size then all the individual files shall be no larger than the requested size. AO-22 If requested, the tool calculates block hashes for a specified block size during an acquisition for each block acquired from the digital source. AO-23 If the tool logs any log significant information, the information is accurately recorded in the log file. AO-24 If the tool executes in a forensically safe execution environment, the digital source is unchanged by the acquisition process.
Tester Name:	mrmw
Test Host:	Joe
Test Date:	Thu Aug 28 14:30:54 2008
Drives:	src(ED-BAD-CPR1) dst (21) other (none)
Source Setup:	No before hash for ED-BAD-CPR1 120103200 total sectors (61492838400 bytes) Drive with known bad sectors Vendor: Maxtor Model: DiamondMax Plus 9 Known Bad Sector List for ED-CPR-BAD-1 Manufacturer: Maxtor Model: 6Y060L0 DiamondMax Plus 9 Serial Number: Y27KR6CE Capacity: 60GB Interface: PATA 54 faulty sectors 10069095, 10069911, 12023808, 18652594, 18656041, 18656857, 18660303, 18661119, 19746716-19746717, 22233904, 23098370, 23383001, 24102466- 24102467, 24104250, 24106656, 24107458, 28959971-28959972, 41825791, 41828995, 52654580, 52655318, 60522984, 68643842-68643843, 69973290, 72714626, 72715293, 82148809, 82148810, 83810525, 85310861, 85313430, 85314038-85314039, 86321211, 86323780, 87186066, 87856313, 87856922, 97191260-97191261, 100093150-100093151, 103861021, 109706975-109706976, 110347947, 110350122-110350123, 115664758, 115835518
Log Highlights:	====== Destination drive setup ====== 195813072 sectors wiped with 21 ====== Comparison of original to clone drive ====== Sectors compared: 120103200 Sectors match: 120103112 Sectors differ: 88 Bytes differ: 45044 Diffs range 10069095-10069096, 10069911-10069912, 12023808-12023809, 18652594-18652595, 18656041-18656042, 18656857-18656858, 18660303-18660304, 18661119-18661120, 19746716-19746717, 22233904-22233905, 23098370-23098371, 23383001-23383002,

```
24102466-24102467, 24104250-24104251, 24106656-24106657,
24107458-24107459, 28959971-28959972, 41825791-41825792,
41828995-41828996, 52654580-52654581, 52655318-52655319,
60522984-60522985, 68643842-68643843, 69973290-69973291,
72714626-72714627, 72715293-72715294, 82148809-82148810,
83810525-83810526, 85310861-85310862, 85313430-85313431,
85314038-85314039, 86321211-86321212, 86323780-86323781,
87186066-87186067, 87856313-87856314, 87856922-87856923,
97191260-97191261, 100093150-100093151, 103861021-103861022,
109706975-109706976, 110347947-110347948, 110350122-110350123,
115664758-115664759, 115835518-115835519
Source (120103200) has 75709872 fewer sectors than destination (195813072)
Zero fill:              0
Src Byte fill (ED):     0
Dst Byte fill (21): 75709872
Other fill:             0
Other no fill:          0
Zero fill range:
Src fill range:
Dst fill range:  120103200-195813071
Other fill range:
Other not filled range:
0 source read errors, 0 destination read errors


====== Tool Settings: ======
avoid yes
write 1
write ? BAD SECTOR ?
simuly yes

Write Block: 32 Tableau Forensic IDE Bridge

====== Extract from X-Ways log.txt file ======
Sectors that could not be read:
10,069,095
10,069,096..10,069,096 skipped.
10,069,911
10,069,912..10,069,912 skipped.
12,023,808
    . . .
115,664,758
115,664,759..115,664,759 skipped.
115,835,518
115,835,519..115,835,519 skipped.

08/29/2008, 10:18:19.1
120,103,112 sector(s) successfully copied.
44 skipped. (Requested skip range was 1 sectors.)
44 bad source sectors encountered.
Corresponding destination sectors filled with:  ? BAD SECTOR ?
====== Summary of Sectors not acquired ======
1 different run lengths observed in 44 runs
44 runs of length 2
88 sectors differ
    0 zero filled and 1 varying non-zero filled
```

Results:

Assertion & Expected Result	Actual Result
AM-01 Source acquired using interface AI.	as expected
AM-02 Source is type DS.	as expected
AM-03 Execution environment is XE.	as expected
AM-05 An image is created on file system type FS.	as expected
AM-06 All visible sectors acquired.	some sectors skipped
AM-08 All sectors accurately acquired.	as expected
AM-09 Error logged.	as expected
AM-10 Benign fill replaces inaccessible sectors.	as expected
AO-01 Image file is complete and accurate.	as expected
AO-05 Multifile image created.	as expected

Test Case DA-09-FW-XP X-Ways 14.8		
	AO-22 Tool calculates hashes by block.	option not available
	AO-23 Logged information is correct.	as expected
	AO-24 Source is unchanged by acquisition.	not checked
Analysis:	Expected results not achieved	

5.2.36　　DA-09-SATA

Test Case DA-09-SATA X-Ways 14.8	
Case Summary:	DA-09 Acquire a digital source that has at least one faulty data sector.
Assertions:	AM-01 The tool uses access interface SRC-AI to access the digital source. AM-02 The tool acquires digital source DS. AM-03 The tool executes in execution environment XE. AM-05 If image file creation is specified, the tool creates an image file on file system type FS. AM-06 All visible sectors are acquired from the digital source. AM-08 All sectors acquired from the digital source are acquired accurately. AM-09 If unresolved errors occur while reading from the selected digital source, the tool notifies the user of the error type and location within the digital source. AM-10 If unresolved errors occur while reading from the selected digital source, the tool uses a benign fill in the destination object in place of the inaccessible data. AO-01 If the tool creates an image file, the data represented by the image file is the same as the data acquired by the tool. AO-05 If the tool creates a multi-file image of a requested size then all the individual files shall be no larger than the requested size. AO-22 If requested, the tool calculates block hashes for a specified block size during an acquisition for each block acquired from the digital source. AO-23 If the tool logs any log significant information, the information is accurately recorded in the log file. AO-24 If the tool executes in a forensically safe execution environment, the digital source is unchanged by the acquisition process.
Tester Name:	mrmw
Test Host:	Freddy
Test Date:	Tue Aug 5 11:54:11 2008
Drives:	src(ED-BAD-CPR4) dst (04-SATA) other (none)
Source Setup:	No before hash for ED-BAD-CPR4 Known Bad Sector List for ED-BAD-CPR4 Manufacturer: Maxtor Model: DiamondMax Plus 9 Serial Number: Y23EGSJE Capacity: 60GB Interface: SATA 35 faulty sectors 6160328, 6160362, 10041157, 10041995, 10118634, 10209448, 11256569, 14115689, 14778391, 14778392, 14778449, 14778479, 14778517, 14778518, 14778519, 14778520, 14778521, 14778551, 14778607, 14778626, 14778627, 14778650, 14778668, 14778669, 14778709, 14778727, 14778747, 14778772, 14778781, 14778870, 14778949, 14778953, 14779038, 14779113, 14779321
Log Highlights:	====== Destination drive setup ====== 156301488 sectors wiped with 4 ====== Comparison of original to clone drive ====== Sectors compared: 120103200 Sectors match: 120103165 Sectors differ: 35 Bytes differ: 17920 Diffs range 6160328, 6160362, 10041157, 10041995, 10118634, 10209448, 11256569, 14115689, 14778391-14778392, 14778449, 14778479, 14778517-14778521, 14778551, 14778607, 14778626-14778627, 14778650, 14778668-14778669, 14778709, 14778727, 14778747, 14778772, 14778781, 14778870, 14778949, 14778953, 14779038, 14779113, 14779321 Source (120103200) has 36198288 fewer sectors than destination (156301488) Zero fill: 0 Src Byte fill (ED): 0

```
Dst Byte fill (04): 36198288
Other fill:                0
Other no fill:             0
Zero fill range:
Src fill range:
Dst fill range:  120103200-156301487
Other fill range:
Other not filled range:
0 source read errors, 0 destination read errors


====== Tool Settings: ======
avoid no
skip NA
write BENIGN
simult yes

OS: Microsoft Windows [Version 5.2.3790]

====== Extract from X-Ways log.txt file ======
Sectors that could not be read:
6,160,328
6,160,362
10,041,157
10,041,995
10,118,634
   . . .
14,778,949
14,778,953
14,779,038
14,779,113
14,779,321


08/06/2008, 01:45:40.5
120,103,165 sector(s) successfully copied.
35 bad source sectors encountered.
Corresponding destination sectors filled with: benign
====== Summary of Sectors not acquired ======
3 different run lengths observed in 28 runs
24 runs of length 1
3 runs of length 2
1 runs of length 5
35 sectors differ
     0 zero filled and 1 varying non-zero filled
```

Results:

Assertion & Expected Result	Actual Result
AM-01 Source acquired using interface AI.	as expected
AM-02 Source is type DS.	as expected
AM-03 Execution environment is XE.	as expected
AM-05 An image is created on file system type FS.	as expected
AM-06 All visible sectors acquired.	as expected
AM-08 All sectors accurately acquired.	as expected
AM-09 Error logged.	as expected
AM-10 Benign fill replaces inaccessible sectors.	as expected
AO-01 Image file is complete and accurate.	as expected
AO-05 Multifile image created.	as expected
AO-22 Tool calculates hashes by block.	option not available
AO-23 Logged information is correct.	as expected
AO-24 Source is unchanged by acquisition.	not checked

Analysis: Expected results achieved

5.2.37 DA-09-USB

Test Case DA-09-USB X-Ways 14.8	
Case Summary:	DA-09 Acquire a digital source that has at least one faulty data sector.
Assertions:	AM-01 The tool uses access interface SRC-AI to access the digital source. AM-02 The tool acquires digital source DS. AM-03 The tool executes in execution environment XE. AM-05 If image file creation is specified, the tool creates an image file on file system type FS. AM-06 All visible sectors are acquired from the digital source. AM-08 All sectors acquired from the digital source are acquired accurately. AM-09 If unresolved errors occur while reading from the selected digital source, the tool notifies the user of the error type and location within the digital source. AM-10 If unresolved errors occur while reading from the selected digital source, the tool uses a benign fill in the destination object in place of the inaccessible data. AO-01 If the tool creates an image file, the data represented by the image file is the same as the data acquired by the tool. AO-05 If the tool creates a multi-file image of a requested size then all the individual files shall be no larger than the requested size. AO-22 If requested, the tool calculates block hashes for a specified block size during an acquisition for each block acquired from the digital source. AO-23 If the tool logs any log significant information, the information is accurately recorded in the log file. AO-24 If the tool executes in a forensically safe execution environment, the digital source is unchanged by the acquisition process.
Tester Name:	mrmw
Test Host:	Frank
Test Date:	Thu Aug 7 08:25:28 2008
Drives:	src(ED-BAD-CPR4) dst (04-SATA) other (none)
Source Setup:	No before hash for ED-BAD-CPR4 Known Bad Sector List for ED-BAD-CPR4 Manufacturer: Maxtor Model: DiamondMax Plus 9 Serial Number: Y23EGSJE Capacity: 60GB Interface: SATA 35 faulty sectors 6160328, 6160362, 10041157, 10041995, 10118634, 10209448, 11256569, 14115689, 14778391, 14778392, 14778449, 14778479, 14778517, 14778518, 14778519, 14778520, 14778521, 14778551, 14778607, 14778626, 14778627, 14778650, 14778668, 14778669, 14778709, 14778727, 14778747, 14778772, 14778781, 14778870, 14778949, 14778953, 14779038, 14779113, 14779321
Log Highlights:	====== Destination drive setup ====== 156301488 sectors wiped with 4 ====== Comparison of original to clone drive ====== Sectors compared: 120103200 Sectors match: 120102474 Sectors differ: 726 Bytes differ: 371712 Diffs range 6160328-6160360, 6160362-6160394, 10041157-10041189, 10041995-10042027, 10118634-10118666, 10209448-10209480, 11256569-11256601, 14115689-14115721, 14778391-14778423, 14778449-14778481, 14778517-14778549, 14778551-14778583, 14778607-14778639, 14778650-14778682, 14778709-14778741, 14778747-14778779, 14778781-14778813, 14778870-14778902, 14778949-14778981, 14779038-14779070, 14779113-14779145, 14779321-14779353 Source (120103200) has 36198288 fewer sectors than destination (156301488)

```
                    Zero fill:               0
                    Src Byte fill (ED):      0
                    Dst Byte fill (04): 36198288
                    Other fill:              0
                    Other no fill:           0
                    Zero fill range:
                    Src fill range:
                    Dst fill range:  120103200-156301487
                    Other fill range:
                    Other not filled range:
                    0 source read errors, 0 destination read errors


                    ====== Tool Settings: ======
                    avoid yes
                    skip 1
                    write benign
                    simult no

                    Write Block: 35 Tableau T3u

                    OS: Microsoft Windows XP [Version 5.1.2600]

                    ====== Extract from X-Ways log.txt file ======
                    Sectors that could not be read:
                    6,160,328
                    6,160,329..6,160,360 skipped.
                    6,160,362
                    6,160,363..6,160,394 skipped.
                    10,041,157
                          . . .
                    14,779,113
                    14,779,114..14,779,145 skipped.
                    14,779,321
                    14,779,322..14,779,353 skipped.


                    08/07/2008, 12:47:36.3
                    120,102,474 sector(s) successfully copied.
                    704 skipped. (Requested skip range was 32 sectors.)
                    22 bad source sectors encountered.
                    Corresponding destination sectors filled with: benign
                    ====== Summary of Sectors not acquired ======
                    1 different run lengths observed in 22 runs
                    22 runs of length 33
                    726 sectors differ
                         0 zero filled and 1 varying non-zero filled
```

Results:	

Assertion & Expected Result	Actual Result
AM-01 Source acquired using interface AI.	as expected
AM-02 Source is type DS.	as expected
AM-03 Execution environment is XE.	as expected
AM-05 An image is created on file system type FS.	as expected
AM-06 All visible sectors acquired.	some sectors skipped
AM-08 All sectors accurately acquired.	as expected
AM-09 Error logged.	as expected
AM-10 Benign fill replaces inaccessible sectors.	as expected
AO-01 Image file is complete and accurate.	as expected
AO-05 Multifile image created.	as expected
AO-22 Tool calculates hashes by block.	option not available
AO-23 Logged information is correct.	as expected
AO-24 Source is unchanged by acquisition.	not checked

Analysis:	Expected results not achieved

5.2.38　DA-13

Test Case DA-13 X-Ways 14.8	
Case Summary:	DA-13 Create an image file where there is insufficient space on a single volume, and use destination device switching to continue on another volume.
Assertions:	AM-01 The tool uses access interface SRC-AI to access the digital source.
	AM-02 The tool acquires digital source DS.
	AM-03 The tool executes in execution environment XE.
	AM-05 If image file creation is specified, the tool creates an image file on file system type FS.
	AM-06 All visible sectors are acquired from the digital source.
	AM-08 All sectors acquired from the digital source are acquired accurately.
	AO-01 If the tool creates an image file, the data represented by the image file is the same as the data acquired by the tool.
	AO-04 If the tool is creating an image file and there is insufficient space on the image destination device to contain the image file, the tool shall notify the user.
	AO-05 If the tool creates a multi-file image of a requested size then all the individual files shall be no larger than the requested size.
	AO-10 If there is insufficient space to contain all files of a multi-file image and if destination device switching is supported, the image is continued on another device.
	AO-22 If requested, the tool calculates block hashes for a specified block size during an acquisition for each block acquired from the digital source.
	AO-23 If the tool logs any log significant information, the information is accurately recorded in the log file.
	AO-24 If the tool executes in a forensically safe execution environment, the digital source is unchanged by the acquisition process.
Tester Name:	mrmw
Test Host:	Frank
Test Date:	Wed Aug 27 08:59:36 2008
Drives:	src(01-IDE) dst (02-IDE) other (8A)
Source Setup:	src hash (SHA1): < A48BB5665D6DC57C22DB68E2F723DA9AA8DF82B9 > src hash (MD5): < F458F673894753FA6A0EC8B8EC63848E > 78165360 total sectors (40020664320 bytes) Model (0BB-00JHC0) serial # (WD-WMAMC74171) <pre>N Start LBA Length Start C/H/S End C/H/S boot Partition type
1 P 000000063 020980827 0000/001/01 1023/254/63   0C Fat32X
2 X 020980890 057175335 1023/000/01 1023/254/63   0F extended
3 S 000000063 000032067 1023/001/01 1023/254/63   01 Fat12
4 x 000032130 002104515 1023/000/01 1023/254/63   05 extended
5 S 000000063 002104452 1023/001/01 1023/254/63   06 Fat16
6 x 002136645 004192965 1023/000/01 1023/254/63   05 extended
7 S 000000063 004192902 1023/001/01 1023/254/63   16 other
8 x 006329610 008401995 1023/000/01 1023/254/63   05 extended
9 S 000000063 008401932 1023/001/01 1023/254/63   0B Fat32
10 x 014731605 010490445 1023/000/01 1023/254/63   05 extended
11 S 000000063 010490382 1023/001/01 1023/254/63   83 Linux
12 x 025222050 004209030 1023/000/01 1023/254/63   05 extended
13 S 000000063 004208967 1023/001/01 1023/254/63   82 Linux swap
14 x 029431080 027744255 1023/000/01 1023/254/63   05 extended
15 S 000000063 027744192 1023/001/01 1023/254/63   07 NTFS
16 S 000000000 000000000 0000/000/00 0000/000/00   00 empty entry
17 P 000000000 000000000 0000/000/00 0000/000/00   00 empty entry
18 P 000000000 000000000 0000/000/00 0000/000/00   00 empty entry
1 020980827 sectors 10742183424 bytes
3 000032067 sectors 16418304 bytes
5 002104452 sectors 1077479424 bytes
7 004192902 sectors 2146765824 bytes
9 008401932 sectors 4301789184 bytes
11 010490382 sectors 5371075584 bytes
13 004208967 sectors 2154991104 bytes
15 027744192 sectors 14205026304 bytes</pre>
Log Highlights:	====== Destination drive setup ====== 39102336 sectors wiped with 8A ====== Tool Settings: ======

Test Case DA-13 X-Ways 14.8	
	size CD (640MB) Write Block: 32 Tableau T5 ====== Extract from X-Ways log.txt file ====== Model: WDC WD400BB-00JHC0 05.0 Total capacity: 40,020,664,320 bytes = 37.3 GB Sector count: 78,165,360 Hash of source data: F458F673894753FA6A0EC8B8EC63848E (MD5)
Results:	

Assertion & Expected Result	Actual Result
AM-01 Source acquired using interface AI.	as expected
AM-02 Source is type DS.	as expected
AM-03 Execution environment is XE.	as expected
AM-05 An image is created on file system type FS.	as expected
AM-06 All visible sectors acquired.	as expected
AM-08 All sectors accurately acquired.	as expected
AO-01 Image file is complete and accurate.	as expected
AO-04 User notified if space exhausted.	as expected
AO-05 Multifile image created.	as expected
AO-10 Image file continued on new device.	as expected
AO-22 Tool calculates hashes by block.	option not available
AO-23 Logged information is correct.	as expected
AO-24 Source is unchanged by acquisition.	not checked

Analysis:	Expected results achieved

5.2.39   DA-14-ATA28

Test Case DA-14-ATA28 X-Ways 14.8	
Case Summary:	DA-14 Create an unaligned clone from an image file.
Assertions:	AM-03 The tool executes in execution environment XE. AO-12 If requested, a clone is created from an image file. AO-13 A clone is created using access interface DST-AI to write to the clone device. AO-14 If an unaligned clone is created, each sector written to the clone is accurately written to the same disk address on the clone that the sector occupied on the digital source. AO-17 If requested, any excess sectors on a clone destination device are not modified. AO-23 If the tool logs any log significant information, the information is accurately recorded in the log file.
Tester Name:	mrmw
Test Host:	Freddy
Test Date:	Mon Jun 30 15:10:51 2008
Drives:	src(43) dst (02-IDE) other (01-FU)
Source Setup:	src hash (SHA256): < 2658F47603DE6B1D883B64823E9733F578658D08D06A4BB8C053C4F57BDC615E > src hash (SHA1): < 888E2E7F7AD237DC7A732281DD93F325065E5871 > src hash (MD5): < BC39C3F7EE7A50E77B9BA1E65A5AEEF7 > 78125000 total sectors (40000000000 bytes) Model (0BB-75JHC0) serial # (WD-WMAMC46588) <pre> N Start LBA Length Start C/H/S End C/H/S boot Partition type 1 P 000000063 020980827 0000/001/01 1023/254/63 0C Fat32X 2 X 020980890 057143205 1023/000/01 1023/254/63 0F extended 3 S 000000063 000032067 1023/001/01 1023/254/63 01 Fat12 4 x 000032130 002104515 1023/000/01 1023/254/63 05 extended 5 S 000000063 002104452 1023/001/01 1023/254/63 06 Fat16 6 x 002136645 004192965 1023/000/01 1023/254/63 05 extended 7 S 000000063 004192902 1023/001/01 1023/254/63 16 other 8 x 006329610 008401995 1023/000/01 1023/254/63 05 extended 9 S 000000063 008401932 1023/001/01 1023/254/63 0B Fat32 10 x 014731605 010490445 1023/000/01 1023/254/63 05 extended 11 S 000000063 010490382 1023/001/01 1023/254/63 83 Linux 12 x 025222050 004209030 1023/000/01 1023/254/63 05 extended 13 S 000000063 004208967 1023/001/01 1023/254/63 82 Linux swap 14 x 029431080 027712125 1023/000/01 1023/254/63 05 extended 15 S 000000063 027712062 1023/001/01 1023/254/63 07 NTFS 16 S 000000000 000000000 0000/000/00 0000/000/00 00 empty entry 17 P 000000000 000000000 0000/000/00 0000/000/00 00 empty entry 18 P 000000000 000000000 0000/000/00 0000/000/00 00 empty entry 1 020980827 sectors 10742183424 bytes 3 000032067 sectors 16418304 bytes 5 002104452 sectors 1077479424 bytes 7 004192902 sectors 2146765824 bytes 9 008401932 sectors 4301789184 bytes 11 010490382 sectors 5371075584 bytes 13 004208967 sectors 2154991104 bytes 15 027712062 sectors 14188575744 bytes</pre>

Log Highlights:	<pre>====== Destination drive setup ======
	78165360 sectors wiped with 2
	
	====== Comparison of original to clone drive ======
	Sectors compared: 78125000
	Sectors match: 78125000
	Sectors differ: 0
	Bytes differ: 0
	Diffs range
	Source (78125000) has 40360 fewer sectors than destination (78165360)
	Zero fill: 0
	Src Byte fill (43): 0
	Dst Byte fill (02): 40360</pre>

```
Other fill:              0
Other no fill:           0
Zero fill range:
Src fill range:
Dst fill range:  78125000-78165359
Other fill range:
Other not filled range:
0 source read errors, 0 destination read errors


====== Tool Settings: ======
fill none
====== Extract from X-Ways log.txt file ======
78,125,000 sector(s) successfully copied.
```

Results:

Assertion & Expected Result	Actual Result
AM-03 Execution environment is XE.	as expected
AO-12 A clone is created from an image file.	as expected
AO-13 Clone created using interface AI.	as expected
AO-14 An unaligned clone is created.	as expected
AO-17 Excess sectors are unchanged.	as expected
AO-23 Logged information is correct.	as expected

Analysis: Expected results achieved

5.2.40   DA-14-ATA48

Test Case DA-14-ATA48 X-Ways 14.8	
Case Summary:	DA-14 Create an unaligned clone from an image file.
Assertions:	AM-03 The tool executes in execution environment XE. AO-12 If requested, a clone is created from an image file. AO-13 A clone is created using access interface DST-AI to write to the clone device. AO-14 If an unaligned clone is created, each sector written to the clone is accurately written to the same disk address on the clone that the sector occupied on the digital source. AO-17 If requested, any excess sectors on a clone destination device are not modified. AO-23 If the tool logs any log significant information, the information is accurately recorded in the log file.
Tester Name:	mrmw
Test Host:	Frank
Test Date:	Tue Jul 1 07:20:43 2008
Drives:	src(4C) dst (29-IDE) other (06-FU)
Source Setup:	src hash (SHA1): < 8FF620D2BEDCCAFE8412EDAAD56C8554F872EFBF > src hash (MD5): < D10F763B56D4CEBA2D1311C61F9FB382 > 390721968 total sectors (200049647616 bytes) 24320/254/63 (max cyl/hd values) 24321/255/63 (number of cyl/hd) IDE disk: Model (WDC WD2000JB-00KFA0) serial # (WD-WMAMR1031111) N Start LBA Length Start C/H/S End C/H/S boot Partition type 1 P 000000063 390700737 0000/001/01 1023/254/63 Boot 07 NTFS 2 P 000000000 000000000 0000/000/00 0000/000/00 00 empty entry 3 P 000000000 000000000 0000/000/00 0000/000/00 00 empty entry 4 P 000000000 000000000 0000/000/00 0000/000/00 00 empty entry 1 390700737 sectors 200038777344 bytes
Log Highlights:	====== Destination drive setup ====== 488397168 sectors wiped with 29 ====== Comparison of original to clone drive ====== Sectors compared: 390721968 Sectors match: 390721968 Sectors differ: 0 Bytes differ: 0 Diffs range Source (390721968) has 97675200 fewer sectors than destination (488397168) Zero fill: 0 Src Byte fill (4C): 0 Dst Byte fill (29): 97675200 Other fill: 0 Other no fill: 0 Zero fill range: Src fill range: Dst fill range: 390721968-488397167 Other fill range: Other not filled range: 0 source read errors, 0 destination read errors ====== Tool Settings: ====== fill none ====== No X-Ways log.txt file created ====== Sectors compared: 390721968 Sectors match: 390721968 Sectors differ: 0
Results:	

Assertion & Expected Result	Actual Result
AM-03 Execution environment is XE.	as expected
AO-12 A clone is created from an image file.	as expected

Test Case DA-14-ATA48 X-Ways 14.8		
	AO-13 Clone created using interface AI.	as expected
	AO-14 An unaligned clone is created.	as expected
	AO-17 Excess sectors are unchanged.	as expected
	AO-23 Logged information is correct.	as expected
Analysis:	Expected results achieved	

5.2.41   DA-14-CF

Test Case DA-14-CF X-Ways 14.8	
Case Summary:	DA-14 Create an unaligned clone from an image file.
Assertions:	AM-03 The tool executes in execution environment XE. AO-12 If requested, a clone is created from an image file. AO-13 A clone is created using access interface DST-AI to write to the clone device. AO-14 If an unaligned clone is created, each sector written to the clone is accurately written to the same disk address on the clone that the sector occupied on the digital source. AO-17 If requested, any excess sectors on a clone destination device are not modified. AO-23 If the tool logs any log significant information, the information is accurately recorded in the log file.
Tester Name:	mrmw
Test Host:	Joe
Test Date:	Tue Jul 1 12:56:51 2008
Drives:	src(C1-CF) dst (C2-CF) other (O1-FU)
Source Setup:	src hash (SHA256): < C7CF0218222DF80D5316511D6814266C7FA507C13F795AD3D323BB73C1590D80 > src hash (SHA1): < 5B8235178DF99FA307430C088F81746606638A0B > src hash (MD5): < 776DF8B4D2589E21DEBCF589EDC16D78 > 503808 total sectors (257949696 bytes)
Log Highlights:	====== Destination drive setup ====== 503808 sectors wiped with C2 ====== Comparison of original to clone drive ====== Sectors compared: 503808 Sectors match: 503807 Sectors differ: 1 Bytes differ: 1 Diffs range 1 0 source read errors, 0 destination read errors ====== Extract from X-Ways log.txt file ====== 503,808 sector(s) successfully copied.
Results:	<table><tr><td>Assertion & Expected Result</td><td>Actual Result</td></tr><tr><td>AM-03 Execution environment is XE.</td><td>as expected</td></tr><tr><td>AO-12 A clone is created from an image file.</td><td>as expected</td></tr><tr><td>AO-13 Clone created using interface AI.</td><td>as expected</td></tr><tr><td>AO-14 An unaligned clone is created.</td><td>one sector differs</td></tr><tr><td>AO-17 Excess sectors are unchanged.</td><td>as expected</td></tr><tr><td>AO-23 Logged information is correct.</td><td>as expected</td></tr></table>
Analysis:	Expected results not achieved

5.2.42 DA-14-F12

Test Case DA-14-F12 X-Ways 14.8	
Case Summary:	DA-14 Create an unaligned clone from an image file.
Assertions:	AM-03 The tool executes in execution environment XE. AO-12 If requested, a clone is created from an image file. AO-13 A clone is created using access interface DST-AI to write to the clone device. AO-14 If an unaligned clone is created, each sector written to the clone is accurately written to the same disk address on the clone that the sector occupied on the digital source. AO-17 If requested, any excess sectors on a clone destination device are not modified. AO-23 If the tool logs any log significant information, the information is accurately recorded in the log file.
Tester Name:	brl
Test Host:	Freddy
Test Date:	Wed Feb 23 12:52:29 2011
Drives:	src(01-IDE) dst (25-SATA) other (06-FU)

Source Setup:	src hash (SHA1): < A48BB5665D6DC57C22DB68E2F723DA9AA8DF82B9 >
	src hash (MD5): < F458F673894753FA6A0EC8B8EC63848E >
	78165360 total sectors (40020664320 bytes)
	Model (0BB-00JHC0) serial # (WD-WMAMC74171)
	<pre>N Start LBA Length Start C/H/S End C/H/S boot Partition type
	 1 P 000000063 020980827 0000/001/01 1023/254/63 0C Fat32X
	 2 X 020980890 057175335 1023/000/01 1023/254/63 0F extended
	 3 S 000000063 000032067 1023/001/01 1023/254/63 01 Fat12
	 4 x 000032130 002104515 1023/000/01 1023/254/63 05 extended
	 5 S 000000063 002104452 1023/001/01 1023/254/63 06 Fat16
	 6 x 002136645 004192965 1023/000/01 1023/254/63 05 extended
	 7 S 000000063 004192902 1023/001/01 1023/254/63 16 other
	 8 x 006329610 008401995 1023/000/01 1023/254/63 05 extended
	 9 S 000000063 008401932 1023/001/01 1023/254/63 0B Fat32
	10 x 014731605 010490445 1023/000/01 1023/254/63 05 extended
	11 S 000000063 010490382 1023/001/01 1023/254/63 83 Linux
	12 x 025222050 004209030 1023/000/01 1023/254/63 05 extended
	13 S 000000063 004208967 1023/001/01 1023/254/63 82 Linux swap
	14 x 029431080 027744255 1023/000/01 1023/254/63 05 extended
	15 S 000000063 027744192 1023/001/01 1023/254/63 07 NTFS
	16 S 000000000 000000000 0000/000/00 0000/000/00 00 empty entry
	17 P 000000000 000000000 0000/000/00 0000/000/00 00 empty entry
	18 P 000000000 000000000 0000/000/00 0000/000/00 00 empty entry
	 1 020980827 sectors 10742183424 bytes
	 3 000032067 sectors 16418304 bytes
	 5 002104452 sectors 1077479424 bytes
	 7 004192902 sectors 2146765824 bytes
	 9 008401932 sectors 4301789184 bytes
	11 010490382 sectors 5371075584 bytes
	13 004208967 sectors 2154991104 bytes
	15 027744192 sectors 14205026304 bytes</pre>

Log Highlights:	====== Destination drive setup ====== 156301488 sectors wiped with 25 ====== Comparison of original to clone drive ====== Sectors compared: 32067 Sectors match: 32067 Sectors differ: 0 Bytes differ: 0 Diffs range: run start Wed Feb 23 13:27:58 2011 run finish Wed Feb 23 13:28:00 2011 elapsed time 0:0:2 Normal exit ====== Tool Settings: ======

Test Case DA-14-F12 X-Ways 14.8	
	fill none ====== Extract from X-Ways log.txt file ====== 32,067 sector(s) successfully copied.
Results:	

Assertion & Expected Result	Actual Result
AM-03 Execution environment is XE.	as expected
AO-12 A clone is created from an image file.	as expected
AO-13 Clone created using interface AI.	as expected
AO-14 An unaligned clone is created.	as expected
AO-17 Excess sectors are unchanged.	as expected
AO-23 Logged information is correct.	as expected

Analysis:	Expected results achieved

5.2.43   DA-14-F16

Test Case DA-14-F16 X-Ways 14.8	
Case Summary:	DA-14 Create an unaligned clone from an image file.
Assertions:	AM-03 The tool executes in execution environment XE. AO-12 If requested, a clone is created from an image file. AO-13 A clone is created using access interface DST-AI to write to the clone device. AO-14 If an unaligned clone is created, each sector written to the clone is accurately written to the same disk address on the clone that the sector occupied on the digital source. AO-17 If requested, any excess sectors on a clone destination device are not modified. AO-23 If the tool logs any log significant information, the information is accurately recorded in the log file.
Tester Name:	brl
Test Host:	Freddy
Test Date:	Wed Feb 23 09:15:08 2011
Drives:	src(43) dst (25-SATA) other (01-FU)

Source Setup:	src hash (SHA256): <
	2658F47603DE6B1D883B64823E9733F578658D08D06A4BB8C053C4F57BDC615E >
	src hash (SHA1): < 888E2E7F7AD237DC7A732281DD93F325065E5871 >
	src hash (MD5): < BC39C3F7EE7A50E77B9BA1E65A5AEEF7 >
	78125000 total sectors (40000000000 bytes)
	Model (0BB-75JHC0) serial # (WD-WMAMC46588)
	
	`N   Start LBA Length     Start C/H/S  End C/H/S    boot Partition type`
	`1 P 000000063 020980827  0000/001/01  1023/254/63       0C Fat32X`
	`2 X 020980890 057143205  1023/000/01  1023/254/63       0F extended`
	`3 S 000000063 000032067  1023/001/01  1023/254/63       01 Fat12`
	`4 x 000032130 002104515  1023/000/01  1023/254/63       05 extended`
	`5 S 000000063 002104452  1023/001/01  1023/254/63       06 Fat16`
	`6 x 002136645 004192965  1023/000/01  1023/254/63       05 extended`
	`7 S 000000063 004192902  1023/001/01  1023/254/63       16 other`
	`8 x 006329610 008401995  1023/000/01  1023/254/63       05 extended`
	`9 S 000000063 008401932  1023/001/01  1023/254/63       0B Fat32`
	`10 x 014731605 010490445  1023/000/01  1023/254/63       05 extended`
	`11 S 000000063 010490382  1023/001/01  1023/254/63       83 Linux`
	`12 x 025222050 004209030  1023/000/01  1023/254/63       05 extended`
	`13 S 000000063 004208967  1023/001/01  1023/254/63       82 Linux swap`
	`14 x 029431080 027712125  1023/000/01  1023/254/63       05 extended`
	`15 S 000000063 027712062  1023/001/01  1023/254/63       07 NTFS`
	`16 S 000000000 000000000  0000/000/00  0000/000/00       00 empty entry`
	`17 P 000000000 000000000  0000/000/00  0000/000/00       00 empty entry`
	`18 P 000000000 000000000  0000/000/00  0000/000/00       00 empty entry`
	`1 020980827 sectors 10742183424 bytes`
	`3 000032067 sectors 16418304 bytes`
	`5 002104452 sectors 1077479424 bytes`
	`7 004192902 sectors 2146765824 bytes`
	`9 008401932 sectors 4301789184 bytes`
	`11 010490382 sectors 5371075584 bytes`
	`13 004208967 sectors 2154991104 bytes`
	`15 027712062 sectors 14188575744 bytes`

Log Highlights:	`====== Destination drive setup ======`
	`156301488 sectors wiped with 25`
	
	`====== Comparison of original to clone drive ======`
	`Sectors compared:       2104452`
	`Sectors match:          2104452`
	`Sectors differ:               0`
	`Bytes differ:                 0`
	`Diffs range:`
	`run start Wed Feb 23 10:05:47 2011`
	`run finish Wed Feb 23 10:06:40 2011`
	`elapsed time 0:0:53`

```
                    Normal exit


                    ====== Tool Settings: ======
                    fill none

                    ====== Extract from X-Ways log.txt file ======
                    2,104,452 sector(s) successfully copied.
```

Results:

Assertion & Expected Result	Actual Result
AM-03 Execution environment is XE.	as expected
AO-12 A clone is created from an image file.	as expected
AO-13 Clone created using interface AI.	as expected
AO-14 An unaligned clone is created.	as expected
AO-17 Excess sectors are unchanged.	as expected
AO-23 Logged information is correct.	as expected

Analysis: Expected results achieved

5.2.44   DA-14-F32

Test Case DA-14-F32 X-Ways 14.8	
Case Summary:	DA-14 Create an unaligned clone from an image file.
Assertions:	AM-03 The tool executes in execution environment XE. AO-12 If requested, a clone is created from an image file. AO-13 A clone is created using access interface DST-AI to write to the clone device. AO-14 If an unaligned clone is created, each sector written to the clone is accurately written to the same disk address on the clone that the sector occupied on the digital source. AO-17 If requested, any excess sectors on a clone destination device are not modified. AO-23 If the tool logs any log significant information, the information is accurately recorded in the log file.
Tester Name:	brl
Test Host:	Freddy
Test Date:	Wed Feb 23 13:43:09 2011
Drives:	src(01-IDE) dst (25-SATA) other (06-FU)
Source Setup:	src hash (SHA1): < A48BB5665D6DC57C22DB68E2F723DA9AA8DF82B9 > src hash (MD5): < F458F673894753FA6A0EC8B8EC63848E > 78165360 total sectors (40020664320 bytes) Model (0BB-00JHC0) serial # (WD-WMAMC74171) <pre> N Start LBA Length Start C/H/S End C/H/S boot Partition type 1 P 000000063 020980827 0000/001/01 1023/254/63 0C Fat32X 2 X 020980890 057175335 1023/000/01 1023/254/63 0F extended 3 S 000000063 000032067 1023/001/01 1023/254/63 01 Fat12 4 x 000032130 002104515 1023/000/01 1023/254/63 05 extended 5 S 000000063 002104452 1023/001/01 1023/254/63 06 Fat16 6 x 002136645 004192965 1023/000/01 1023/254/63 05 extended 7 S 000000063 004192902 1023/001/01 1023/254/63 16 other 8 x 006329610 008401995 1023/000/01 1023/254/63 05 extended 9 S 000000063 008401932 1023/001/01 1023/254/63 0B Fat32 10 x 014731605 010490445 1023/000/01 1023/254/63 05 extended 11 S 000000063 010490382 1023/001/01 1023/254/63 83 Linux 12 x 025222050 004209030 1023/000/01 1023/254/63 05 extended 13 S 000000063 004208967 1023/001/01 1023/254/63 82 Linux swap 14 x 029431080 027744255 1023/000/01 1023/254/63 05 extended 15 S 000000063 027744192 1023/001/01 1023/254/63 07 NTFS 16 S 000000000 000000000 0000/000/00 0000/000/00 00 empty entry 17 P 000000000 000000000 0000/000/00 0000/000/00 00 empty entry 18 P 000000000 000000000 0000/000/00 0000/000/00 00 empty entry 1 020980827 sectors 10742183424 bytes 3 000032067 sectors 16418304 bytes 5 002104452 sectors 1077479424 bytes 7 004192902 sectors 2146765824 bytes 9 008401932 sectors 4301789184 bytes 11 010490382 sectors 5371075584 bytes 13 004208967 sectors 2154991104 bytes 15 027744192 sectors 14205026304 bytes</pre>
Log Highlights:	====== Destination drive setup ====== 156301488 sectors wiped with 25 ====== Comparison of original to clone drive ====== Sectors compared: 8401932 Sectors match: 8401929 Sectors differ: 3 Bytes differ: 3 Diffs range: 1, 36, 8226 Source (8401932) has 819315 fewer sectors than destination (9221247) Zero fill: 0 Src Byte fill (01): 0 Dst Byte fill (25): 819315 Other fill: 0 Other no fill: 0 Zero fill range:

```
Test Case DA-14-F32 X-Ways 14.8
              Src fill range:
              Dst fill range:  8401932-9221246
              Other fill range:
              Other not filled range:
              run start Wed Feb 23 14:10:22 2011
              run finish Wed Feb 23 14:13:53 2011
              elapsed time 0:3:31
              Normal exit


              ====== Tool Settings: ======
              fill none

              ====== Extract from X-Ways log.txt file ======
              8,401,932 sector(s) successfully copied.

Results:
```

Assertion & Expected Result	Actual Result
AM-03 Execution environment is XE.	as expected
AO-12 A clone is created from an image file.	as expected
AO-13 Clone created using interface AI.	as expected
AO-14 An unaligned clone is created.	three sectors differ
AO-17 Excess sectors are unchanged.	as expected
AO-23 Logged information is correct.	as expected

```
Analysis:     Expected results not achieved
```

5.2.45   DA-14-F32X

Test Case DA-14-F32X X-Ways 14.8	
Case Summary:	DA-14 Create an unaligned clone from an image file.
Assertions:	AM-03 The tool executes in execution environment XE. AO-12 If requested, a clone is created from an image file. AO-13 A clone is created using access interface DST-AI to write to the clone device. AO-14 If an unaligned clone is created, each sector written to the clone is accurately written to the same disk address on the clone that the sector occupied on the digital source. AO-17 If requested, any excess sectors on a clone destination device are not modified. AO-23 If the tool logs any log significant information, the information is accurately recorded in the log file.
Tester Name:	brl
Test Host:	Freddy
Test Date:	Wed Feb 23 10:14:26 2011
Drives:	src(43) dst (25-SATA) other (01-FU)
Source Setup:	src hash (SHA256): < 2658F47603DE6B1D883B64823E9733F578658D08D06A4BB8C053C4F57BDC615E > src hash (SHA1): < 888E2E7F7AD237DC7A732281DD93F325065E5871 > src hash (MD5): < BC39C3F7EE7A50E77B9BA1E65A5AEEF7 > 78125000 total sectors (40000000000 bytes) Model (0BB-75JHC0) serial # (WD-WMAMC46588) <pre> N Start LBA Length Start C/H/S End C/H/S boot Partition type 1 P 000000063 020980827 0000/001/01 1023/254/63 0C Fat32X 2 X 020980890 057143205 1023/000/01 1023/254/63 0F extended 3 S 000000063 000032067 1023/001/01 1023/254/63 01 Fat12 4 x 000032130 002104515 1023/000/01 1023/254/63 05 extended 5 S 000000063 002104452 1023/001/01 1023/254/63 06 Fat16 6 x 002136645 004192965 1023/000/01 1023/254/63 05 extended 7 S 000000063 004192902 1023/001/01 1023/254/63 16 other 8 x 006329610 008401995 1023/000/01 1023/254/63 05 extended 9 S 000000063 008401932 1023/001/01 1023/254/63 0B Fat32 10 x 014731605 010490445 1023/000/01 1023/254/63 05 extended 11 S 000000063 010490382 1023/001/01 1023/254/63 83 Linux 12 x 025222050 004209030 1023/000/01 1023/254/63 05 extended 13 S 000000063 004208967 1023/001/01 1023/254/63 82 Linux swap 14 x 029431080 027712125 1023/000/01 1023/254/63 05 extended 15 S 000000063 027712062 1023/001/01 1023/254/63 07 NTFS 16 S 000000000 000000000 0000/000/00 0000/000/00 00 empty entry 17 P 000000000 000000000 0000/000/00 0000/000/00 00 empty entry 18 P 000000000 000000000 0000/000/00 0000/000/00 00 empty entry 1 020980827 sectors 10742183424 bytes 3 000032067 sectors 16418304 bytes 5 002104452 sectors 1077479424 bytes 7 004192902 sectors 2146765824 bytes 9 008401932 sectors 4301789184 bytes 11 010490382 sectors 5371075584 bytes 13 004208967 sectors 2154991104 bytes 15 027712062 sectors 14188575744 bytes</pre>

Log Highlights:	<pre>====== Destination drive setup ======
	156301488 sectors wiped with 25
	
	====== Comparison of original to clone drive ======
	Sectors compared: 20980827
	Sectors match: 20980824
	Sectors differ: 3
	Bytes differ: 3
	Diffs range: 1, 32, 10268
	Source (20980827) has 1558305 fewer sectors than destination (22539132)
	Zero fill: 0
	Src Byte fill (43): 0
	Dst Byte fill (25): 1558305</pre>

```
Test Case DA-14-F32X X-Ways 14.8
                Other fill:     0
                Other no fill: 0
                Zero fill range:
                Src fill range:
                Dst fill range:  20980827-22539131
                Other fill range:
                Other not filled range:
                run start Wed Feb 23 11:31:41 2011
                run finish Wed Feb 23 11:40:21 2011
                elapsed time 0:8:40
                Normal exit


                ====== Tool Settings: ======
                fill none

                ====== Extract from X-Ways log.txt file ======
                20,980,827 sector(s) successfully copied.
```

Results:		
	Assertion & Expected Result	**Actual Result**
	AO-03 Execution environment is XE.	as expected
	AO-12 A clone is created from an image file.	as expected
	AO-13 Clone created using interface AI.	as expected
	AO-14 An unaligned clone is created.	three sectors differ
	AO-17 Excess sectors are unchanged.	as expected
	AO-23 Logged information is correct.	as expected

Analysis:	Expected results not achieved

5.2.46   DA-14-FLOPPY

Test Case DA-14-FLOPPY X-Ways 14.8	
Case Summary:	DA-14 Create an unaligned clone from an image file.
Assertions:	AM-03 The tool executes in execution environment XE. AO-12 If requested, a clone is created from an image file. AO-13 A clone is created using access interface DST-AI to write to the clone device. AO-14 If an unaligned clone is created, each sector written to the clone is accurately written to the same disk address on the clone that the sector occupied on the digital source. AO-17 If requested, any excess sectors on a clone destination device are not modified. AO-23 If the tool logs any log significant information, the information is accurately recorded in the log file.
Tester Name:	mrmw
Test Host:	Frank
Test Date:	Mon Jun 30 09:19:32 2008
Drives:	src(floppy) dst (floppy2) other (01-FU)
Source Setup:	src hash (SHA1): < e2863334ac7eaabc7c8a0d62eb0d3b3af29f2c40 > src hash (MD5): < 17f6a5925be2f38eedaf435ff8b6a6f4 > Floppy disk
Log Highlights:	====== Destination drive setup ====== 2880 sectors wiped with 1 Comparison of src (/def/fd0) to restored floppy (/dev/sdh) md5sum /dev/fd0 17f6a5925be2f38eedaf435ff8b6a6f4 /dev/fd0 md5sum /dev/sdh 17f6a5925be2f38eedaf435ff8b6a6f4 /dev/sdh ====== Extract from X-Ways log.txt file ====== 2,880 sector(s) successfully copied. ****** NO CMP File ******
Results:	

Assertion & Expected Result	Actual Result
AM-03 Execution environment is XE.	as expected
AO-12 A clone is created from an image file.	as expected
AO-13 Clone created using interface AI.	as expected
AO-14 An unaligned clone is created.	as expected
AO-17 Excess sectors are unchanged.	as expected
AO-23 Logged information is correct.	as expected

Analysis:	Expected results achieved

5.2.47   DA-14-NTFS

Test Case DA-14-NTFS X-Ways 14.8	
Case Summary:	DA-14 Create an unaligned clone from an image file.
Assertions:	AM-03 The tool executes in execution environment XE. AO-12 If requested, a clone is created from an image file. AO-13 A clone is created using access interface DST-AI to write to the clone device. AO-14 If an unaligned clone is created, each sector written to the clone is accurately written to the same disk address on the clone that the sector occupied on the digital source. AO-17 If requested, any excess sectors on a clone destination device are not modified. AO-23 If the tool logs any log significant information, the information is accurately recorded in the log file.
Tester Name:	Frank
Test Host:	mrmw
Test Date:	Wed Jul 23 08:58:48 2008
Drives:	src(01-IDE) dst (07-IDE) other (none)
Source Setup:	src hash (SHA1): < A48BB5665D6DC57C22DB68E2F723DA9AA8DF82B9 > src hash (MD5): < F458F673894753FA6A0EC8B8EC63848E > 78165360 total sectors (40020664320 bytes) Model (0BB-00JHC0) serial # (WD-WMAMC74171) <pre>N Start LBA Length Start C/H/S End C/H/S boot Partition type
1 P 000000063 020980827 0000/001/01 1023/254/63   0C Fat32X
2 X 020980890 057175335 1023/000/01 1023/254/63   0F extended
3 S 000000063 000032067 1023/001/01 1023/254/63   01 Fat12
4 x 000032130 002104515 1023/000/01 1023/254/63   05 extended
5 S 000000063 002104452 1023/001/01 1023/254/63   06 Fat16
6 x 002136645 004192965 1023/000/01 1023/254/63   05 extended
7 S 000000063 004192902 1023/001/01 1023/254/63   16 other
8 x 006329610 008401995 1023/000/01 1023/254/63   05 extended
9 S 000000063 008401932 1023/001/01 1023/254/63   0B Fat32
10 x 014731605 010490445 1023/000/01 1023/254/63   05 extended
11 S 000000063 010490382 1023/001/01 1023/254/63   83 Linux
12 x 025222050 004209030 1023/000/01 1023/254/63   05 extended
13 S 000000063 004208967 1023/001/01 1023/254/63   82 Linux swap
14 x 029431080 027744255 1023/000/01 1023/254/63   05 extended
15 S 000000063 027744192 1023/001/01 1023/254/63   07 NTFS
16 S 000000000 000000000 0000/000/00 0000/000/00   00 empty entry
17 P 000000000 000000000 0000/000/00 0000/000/00   00 empty entry
18 P 000000000 000000000 0000/000/00 0000/000/00   00 empty entry</pre>1 020980827 sectors 10742183424 bytes 3 000032067 sectors 16418304 bytes 5 002104452 sectors 1077479424 bytes 7 004192902 sectors 2146765824 bytes 9 008401932 sectors 4301789184 bytes 11 010490382 sectors 5371075584 bytes 13 004208967 sectors 2154991104 bytes 15 027744192 sectors 14205026304 bytes 01F12-md5 16418303 E20E3CFEA80BF6F2D2AA75E829CC8CD9 01F12-sha1 16418303 F8B72B65436DE3BD394ACFF71D405D0389C0E9B7
Log Highlights:	====== Comparison of original to clone drive ====== Sectors compared: 27744192 Sectors match: 27743958 Sectors differ: 234 Bytes differ: 51360 Diffs range: 6160368-6160390, 6160392-6160398, 6160424-6160479, 6291448, 6291456-6291479, 6291504-6291519, 9759488, 9760000, 13872088-13872135, 13872168-13872175, 13872615, 13928328-13928367, 27744184-27744191 Source (27744192) has 112455 fewer sectors than destination (27856647) Zero fill: 539 Src Byte fill (01): 111007 Dst Byte fill (07): 62

```
Other fill:     0
Other no fill: 847
Zero fill range:  27744257-27744510, 27744512-27744765,
27744767-27744797
Src fill range:  27744798-27744806, 27744828-27744870,
27744892-27744934, 27744956-27744998, 27745020-27745062,
27745084-27745126, 27745148-27745190, 27745212-27745254,
27745276-27745318, 27745340-27745382, 27745404-27745446,
27745468-27745510, 27745532-27745574, 27745596-27745638,
27745660-27745702, 27745724-27745766, 27745788-27745830,
27745852-27745894, 27745916-27745958, 27745980-27746022. . . + 110181 more
Dst fill range:  27744193-27744254
Other fill range:
Other not filled range:  27744192, 27744255-27744256,
27744511, 27744766, 27744807-27744827, 27744871-27744891,
27744935-27744955, 27744999-27745019, 27745063-27745083,
27745127-27745147, 27745191-27745211, 27745255-27745275,
27745319-27745339, 27745383-27745403, 27745447-27745467,
27745511-27745531, 27745575-27745595, 27745639-27745659,
27745703-27745723, 27745767-27745787. . . + 506 more
run start Thu Jul 24 07:27:13 2008
run finish Thu Jul 24 07:57:38 2008
elapsed time 0:30:25
Normal exit

====== Excess Destination Sectors Hashes ======
Hash Before restore:
MD5  14205022208 - 14262603263 = 1B6727BB9E6F313A5697377413DDD58F
Hash after restore:
MD5  14205022208 - 14262603263 = 1B6727BB9E6F313A5697377413DDD58F

====== Tool Settings: ======
fill none

====== Extract from X-Ways log.txt file ======
27,744,184 sector(s) successfully copied.
```

Results:

Assertion & Expected Result	Actual Result
AM-03 Execution environment is XE.	as expected
AO-12 A clone is created from an image file.	as expected
AO-13 Clone created using interface AI.	as expected
AO-14 An unaligned clone is created.	some sectors differ
AO-17 Excess sectors are unchanged.	as expected
AO-23 Logged information is correct.	as expected

Analysis: Expected results not achieved

5.2.48 DA-14-SCSI

Test Case DA-14-SCSI X-Ways 14.8	
Case Summary:	DA-14 Create an unaligned clone from an image file.
Assertions:	AM-03 The tool executes in execution environment XE. AO-12 If requested, a clone is created from an image file. AO-13 A clone is created using access interface DST-AI to write to the clone device. AO-14 If an unaligned clone is created, each sector written to the clone is accurately written to the same disk address on the clone that the sector occupied on the digital source. AO-17 If requested, any excess sectors on a clone destination device are not modified. AO-23 If the tool logs any log significant information, the information is accurately recorded in the log file.
Tester Name:	mrmw
Test Host:	Freddy
Test Date:	Mon Aug 4 08:29:42 2008
Drives:	src(E0) dst (E4) other (none)
Source Setup:	src hash (SHA1): < 4A6941F1337A8A22B10FC844B4D7FA6158BECB82 > src hash (MD5): < A97C8F36B7AC9D5233B90AC09284F938 > 17938985 total sectors (9184760320 bytes) Model (ATLAS10K2-TY092J) serial # (169028142436)
Log Highlights:	====== Destination drive setup ====== 17938985 sectors wiped with E4 ====== Comparison of original to clone drive ====== Sectors compared: 17938985 Sectors match: 17938985 Sectors differ: 0 Bytes differ: 0 Diffs range 0 source read errors, 0 destination read errors ====== Tool Settings: ====== none fill ====== Extract from X-Ways log.txt file ====== 17,938,985 sector(s) successfully copied.
Results:	

Assertion & Expected Result	Actual Result
AM-03 Execution environment is XE.	as expected
AO-12 A clone is created from an image file.	as expected
AO-13 Clone created using interface AI.	as expected
AO-14 An unaligned clone is created.	as expected
AO-17 Excess sectors are unchanged.	as expected
AO-23 Logged information is correct.	as expected

Analysis:	Expected results achieved

5.2.49   DA-14-SATA28

Test Case DA-14-SATA28 X-Ways 14.8	
Case Summary:	DA-14 Create an unaligned clone from an image file.
Assertions:	AM-03 The tool executes in execution environment XE. AO-12 If requested, a clone is created from an image file. AO-13 A clone is created using access interface DST-AI to write to the clone device. AO-14 If an unaligned clone is created, each sector written to the clone is accurately written to the same disk address on the clone that the sector occupied on the digital source. AO-17 If requested, any excess sectors on a clone destination device are not modified. AO-23 If the tool logs any log significant information, the information is accurately recorded in the log file.
Tester Name:	brl
Test Host:	Freddy
Test Date:	Tue Feb 15 15:53:36 2011
Drives:	src(01-SATA) dst (04-SATA) other (3E-SATA)
Source Setup:	src hash (SHA256): < 1AA01FEAE55F5CD55185D2B1A1359B3F913E7093FEF1D1ADA220CAC456BA40D8 > src hash (SHA1): < 4951236428C36B944E62E8D65862DCBEF05F282C > src hash (MD5): < 0A49B13D91FA9DA87CEEE9D006CB6FD6 > 156301488 total sectors (80026361856 bytes) Model (0JD-32HKA0) serial # (WD-WMAJ91448529)
Log Highlights:	====== Destination drive setup ====== 156301488 sectors wiped with 4 ====== Comparison of original to clone drive ====== Sectors compared: 156301488 Sectors match: 156301488 Sectors differ: 0 Bytes differ: 0 Diffs range 0 source read errors, 0 destination read errors ====== Tool Settings: ====== fill none ====== Extract from X-Ways log.txt file ====== 156,301,488 sector(s) successfully copied.
Results:	

Assertion & Expected Result	Actual Result
AM-03 Execution environment is XE.	as expected
AO-12 A clone is created from an image file.	as expected
AO-13 Clone created using interface AI.	as expected
AO-14 An unaligned clone is created.	as expected
AO-17 Excess sectors are unchanged.	as expected
AO-23 Logged information is correct.	as expected

Analysis:	Expected results achieved

5.2.50 DA-14-SATA48

Test Case DA-14-SATA48 X-Ways 14.8	
Case Summary:	DA-14 Create an unaligned clone from an image file.
Assertions:	AM-03 The tool executes in execution environment XE. AO-12 If requested, a clone is created from an image file. AO-13 A clone is created using access interface DST-AI to write to the clone device. AO-14 If an unaligned clone is created, each sector written to the clone is accurately written to the same disk address on the clone that the sector occupied on the digital source. AO-17 If requested, any excess sectors on a clone destination device are not modified. AO-23 If the tool logs any log significant information, the information is accurately recorded in the log file.
Tester Name:	brl
Test Host:	Freddy
Test Date:	Wed Feb 16 13:11:51 2011
Drives:	src(0B-SATA) dst (46-SATA) other (3E-SATA)
Source Setup:	src hash (SHA1): < DA892EE968DD828F2F1B6825C1D3EF35062A0737 > src hash (MD5): < 1873847F597A69D0F5DB991B67E84F92 > 488397168 total sectors (250059350016 bytes) 30400/254/63 (max cyl/hd values) 30401/255/63 (number of cyl/hd) Model (00JD-22FYB0) serial # (WD-WMAEH2677545)
Log Highlights:	====== Destination drive setup ====== 488397168 sectors wiped with 46 ====== Comparison of original to clone drive ====== Sectors compared: 488397168 Sectors match: 488397168 Sectors differ: 0 Bytes differ: 0 Diffs range 0 source read errors, 0 destination read errors ====== Tool Settings: ====== fill none ====== Extract from X-Ways log.txt file ====== 488,397,168 sector(s) successfully copied.
Results:	

Assertion & Expected Result	Actual Result
AM-03 Execution environment is XE.	as expected
AO-12 A clone is created from an image file.	as expected
AO-13 Clone created using interface AI.	as expected
AO-14 An unaligned clone is created.	as expected
AO-17 Excess sectors are unchanged.	as expected
AO-23 Logged information is correct.	as expected

Analysis:	Expected results achieved

5.2.51   DA-14-THUMB

Test Case DA-14-THUMB X-Ways 14.8	
Case Summary:	DA-14 Create an unaligned clone from an image file.
Assertions:	AM-03 The tool executes in execution environment XE. AO-12 If requested, a clone is created from an image file. AO-13 A clone is created using access interface DST-AI to write to the clone device. AO-14 If an unaligned clone is created, each sector written to the clone is accurately written to the same disk address on the clone that the sector occupied on the digital source. AO-17 If requested, any excess sectors on a clone destination device are not modified. AO-23 If the tool logs any log significant information, the information is accurately recorded in the log file.
Tester Name:	brl
Test Host:	Freddy
Test Date:	Fri Feb 11 10:47:03 2011
Drives:	src(D5-THUMB) dst (D6-THUMB) other (3E-SATA)
Source Setup:	src hash (SHA1): < D68520EF74A336E49DCCF83815B7B08FDC53E38A > src hash (MD5): < C843593624B2B3B878596D8760B19954 > 505856 total sectors (258998272 bytes) Model (usb2.0Flash Disk) serial # ()
Log Highlights:	====== Destination drive setup ====== 4001760 sectors wiped with D6 ====== Comparison of original to clone drive ====== Sectors compared: 505856 Sectors match: 505856 Sectors differ: 0 Bytes differ: 0 Diffs range Source (505856) has 3495904 fewer sectors than destination (4001760) Zero fill: 0 Src Byte fill (D5): 0 Dst Byte fill (D6): 3495904 Other fill: 0 Other no fill: 0 Zero fill range: Src fill range: Dst fill range: 505856-4001759 Other fill range: Other not filled range: 0 source read errors, 0 destination read errors ====== Tool Settings: ====== fill none ====== Extract from X-Ways log.txt file ====== 505,856 sector(s) successfully copied. 505,856 sector(s) successfully copied.
Results:	

Assertion & Expected Result	Actual Result
AM-03 Execution environment is XE.	as expected
AO-12 A clone is created from an image file.	as expected
AO-13 Clone created using interface AI.	as expected
AO-14 An unaligned clone is created.	as expected
AO-17 Excess sectors are unchanged.	as expected
AO-23 Logged information is correct.	as expected

Analysis:	Expected results achieved

5.2.52   DA-14-USB

Test Case DA-14-USB X-Ways 14.8	
Case Summary:	DA-14 Create an unaligned clone from an image file.
Assertions:	AM-03 The tool executes in execution environment XE. AO-12 If requested, a clone is created from an image file. AO-13 A clone is created using access interface DST-AI to write to the clone device. AO-14 If an unaligned clone is created, each sector written to the clone is accurately written to the same disk address on the clone that the sector occupied on the digital source. AO-17 If requested, any excess sectors on a clone destination device are not modified. AO-23 If the tool logs any log significant information, the information is accurately recorded in the log file.
Tester Name:	mrmw
Test Host:	Frank
Test Date:	Mon Aug 4 11:17:05 2008
Drives:	src (63-FU2) dst (61-FU2) other (none)
Source Setup:	src hash (SHA256): < EC8EF011494BA6DA18F74C47547C3E74E7180585096A830F9247A98EF613BB1D > src hash (SHA1): < F7069EDCBEAC863C88DECED82159F22DA96BE99B > src hash (MD5): < EE217BC4FA4F3D1B4021D29B065AA9EC > 117304992 total sectors (60060155904 bytes) Model (SP0612N) serial # () N Start LBA Length Start C/H/S End C/H/S boot Partition type 1 P 000000063 004192902 0000/001/01 0260/254/63 Boot 06 Fat16 2 X 004192965 113097600 0261/000/01 1023/254/63 0F extended 3 S 000000063 113097537 0261/001/01 1023/254/63 0B Fat32 4 S 000000000 000000000 0000/000/00 0000/000/00 00 empty entry 5 P 000000000 000000000 0000/000/00 0000/000/00 00 empty entry 6 P 000000000 000000000 0000/000/00 0000/000/00 00 empty entry 1 004192902 sectors 2146765824 bytes 3 113097537 sectors 57905938944 bytes
Log Highlights:	====== Destination drive setup ====== 117304992 sectors wiped with 63 ====== Comparison of original to clone drive ====== Sectors compared: 117304992 Sectors match: 117304992 Sectors differ: 0 Bytes differ: 0 Diffs range 0 source read errors, 0 destination read errors ====== Extract from X-Ways log.txt file ====== 117,304,992 sector(s) successfully copied.
Results:	

Assertion & Expected Result	Actual Result
AM-03 Execution environment is XE.	as expected
AO-12 A clone is created from an image file.	as expected
AO-13 Clone created using interface AI.	as expected
AO-14 An unaligned clone is created.	as expected
AO-17 Excess sectors are unchanged.	as expected
AO-23 Logged information is correct.	as expected

Analysis:	Expected results achieved

5.2.53 DA-17

Test Case DA-17 X-Ways 14.8	
Case Summary:	DA-17 Create a truncated clone from an image file.
Assertions:	AM-03 The tool executes in execution environment XE. AO-12 If requested, a clone is created from an image file. AO-13 A clone is created using access interface DST-AI to write to the clone device. AO-19 If there is insufficient space to create a complete clone, a truncated clone is created using all available sectors of the clone device. AO-20 If a truncated clone is created, the tool notifies the user. AO-23 If the tool logs any log significant information, the information is accurately recorded in the log file.
Tester Name:	mrmw
Test Host:	Joe
Test Date:	Thu Aug 28 10:03:50 2008
Drives:	src(43) dst (8F) other (01-FU)

Source Setup:	src hash (SHA256): <
	2658F47603DE6B1D883B64823E9733F578658D08D06A4BB8C053C4F57BDC615E >
	src hash (SHA1): < 888E2E7F7AD237DC7A732281DD93F325065E5871 >
	src hash (MD5): < BC39C3F7EE7A50E77B9BA1E65A5AEEF7 >
	78125000 total sectors (40000000000 bytes)
	Model (0BB-75JHC0) serial # (WD-WMAMC46588)
	  N Start LBA Length Start C/H/S End C/H/S boot Partition type
	  1 P 000000063 020980827 0000/001/01 1023/254/63 0C Fat32X
	  2 X 020980890 057143205 1023/000/01 1023/254/63 0F extended
	  3 S 000000063 000032067 1023/001/01 1023/254/63 01 Fat12
	  4 x 000032130 002104515 1023/000/01 1023/254/63 05 extended
	  5 S 000000063 002104452 1023/001/01 1023/254/63 06 Fat16
	  6 x 002136645 004192965 1023/000/01 1023/254/63 05 extended
	  7 S 000000063 004192902 1023/001/01 1023/254/63 16 other
	  8 x 006329610 008401995 1023/000/01 1023/254/63 05 extended
	  9 S 000000063 008401932 1023/001/01 1023/254/63 0B Fat32
	 10 x 014731605 010490445 1023/000/01 1023/254/63 05 extended
	 11 S 000000063 010490382 1023/001/01 1023/254/63 83 Linux
	 12 x 025222050 004209030 1023/000/01 1023/254/63 05 extended
	 13 S 000000063 004208967 1023/001/01 1023/254/63 82 Linux swap
	 14 x 029431080 027712125 1023/000/01 1023/254/63 05 extended
	 15 S 000000063 027712062 1023/001/01 1023/254/63 07 NTFS
	 16 S 000000000 000000000 0000/000/00 0000/000/00 00 empty entry
	 17 P 000000000 000000000 0000/000/00 0000/000/00 00 empty entry
	 18 P 000000000 000000000 0000/000/00 0000/000/00 00 empty entry
	 1 020980827 sectors 10742183424 bytes
	 3 000032067 sectors 16418304 bytes
	 5 002104452 sectors 1077479424 bytes
	 7 004192902 sectors 2146765824 bytes
	 9 008401932 sectors 4301789184 bytes
	11 010490382 sectors 5371075584 bytes
	13 004208967 sectors 2154991104 bytes
	15 027712062 sectors 14188575744 bytes

Log Highlights:	====== Destination drive setup ====== 39102336 sectors wiped with 8F ====== No X-Ways log.txt file created ====== ****** INSERT MESSAGE HERE ****** add dst info
Results:	

Assertion & Expected Result	Actual Result
AM-03 Execution environment is XE.	as expected
AO-12 A clone is created from an image file.	as expected
AO-13 Clone created using interface AI.	as expected
AO-19 Truncated clone is created.	as expected
AO-20 User notified that clone is truncated.	as expected
AO-23 Logged information is correct.	as expected

Test Case DA-17 X-Ways 14.8	
Analysis:	Expected results achieved

About the National Institute of Justice

A component of the Office of Justice Programs, NIJ is the research, development and evaluation agency of the U.S. Department of Justice. NIJ's mission is to advance scientific research, development and evaluation to enhance the administration of justice and public safety. NIJ's principal authorities are derived from the Omnibus Crime Control and Safe Streets Act of 1968, as amended (see 42 U.S.C. §§ 3721–3723).

The NIJ Director is appointed by the President and confirmed by the Senate. The Director establishes the Institute's objectives, guided by the priorities of the Office of Justice Programs, the U.S. Department of Justice, and the needs of the field. The Institute actively solicits the views of criminal justice and other professionals and researchers to inform its search for the knowledge and tools to guide policy and practice.

Strategic Goals

NIJ has seven strategic goals grouped into three categories:

Creating relevant knowledge and tools

1. Partner with state and local practitioners and policymakers to identify social science research and technology needs.
2. Create scientific, relevant, and reliable knowledge—with a particular emphasis on terrorism, violent crime, drugs and crime, cost-effectiveness, and community-based efforts—to enhance the administration of justice and public safety.
3. Develop affordable and effective tools and technologies to enhance the administration of justice and public safety.

Dissemination

4. Disseminate relevant knowledge and information to practitioners and policymakers in an understandable, timely and concise manner.
5. Act as an honest broker to identify the information, tools and technologies that respond to the needs of stakeholders.

Agency management

6. Practice fairness and openness in the research and development process.
7. Ensure professionalism, excellence, accountability, cost-effectiveness and integrity in the management and conduct of NIJ activities and programs.

Program Areas

In addressing these strategic challenges, the Institute is involved in the following program areas: crime control and prevention, including policing; drugs and crime; justice systems and offender behavior, including corrections; violence and victimization; communications and information technologies; critical incident response; investigative and forensic sciences, including DNA; less-than-lethal technologies; officer protection; education and training technologies; testing and standards; technology assistance to law enforcement and corrections agencies; field testing of promising programs; and international crime control.

In addition to sponsoring research and development and technology assistance, NIJ evaluates programs, policies, and technologies. NIJ communicates its research and evaluation findings through conferences and print and electronic media.

To find out more about the National Institute of Justice, please visit:

www.nij.gov

or contact:

National Criminal Justice
 Reference Service
P.O. Box 6000
Rockville, MD 20849–6000
800–851–3420
http://www.ncjrs.gov